THE

FOREST TREE CULTURIST:

ON THE CULTIVATION OF

AMERICAN FOREST TREES,

WITH NOTES ON

THE MOST VALUABLE FOREIGN SPECIES

BY

ANDREW S. FULLER,

Horticulturist,

AUTHOR OF "THE GRAPE CULTURIST," "STRAWBERRY CULTURIST," ETC., ETC.

NEW YORK:

THE AMERICAN NEWS COMPANY,

39 AND 41 CHAMBERS STREET.

PREFACE.

Some years since, while gratifying my taste for Horticultural experiments, I was led to plant seeds of many of our native forest trees. The results satisfied me that nothing was wanting but a better acquaintance with the nature and habits of these seeds to insure success with them as uniformly as with any others; consequently I gave the subject attention, and by observation and experiment learned how to manage not only the trees of our own forests, but many foreign varieties. I would not be understood to say that I have planted seeds and raised trees of every *species* and *variety*, but have experimented sufficiently with the different *species* as to know whereof I write. My success was such that the Farmers' Club of the American Institute desired me to give at one of their meetings an account of my experiments, which I did briefly. This was published as a portion of the Report of the meeting in the New York *Tribune*, and from that copied by other papers throughout the country. In consequence thereof, I have received many letters asking more definite information on different points, so many that I have been unable to reply to them so fully as I could have wished.

The following pages were written for the purpose of giving such information as the public seem to desire. I have avoided, so far as I could, the use of botanical and scientific terms, having written, not for professional horticulturists and men of science, but for practical farmers. I have therefore endeavored to give the *how* rather than the *why*, the practical rather than the theoretical. The man of letters will also undoubtedly find much to criticise in the literary character of the book; this fault I regret more than others can; but if I have so expressed myself that the reader can get my meaning, I shall be content. The book was written for the purpose of showing others how to benefit themselves, and while doing it to conduce to the wealth of the country. If it shall aid in awaking a more general interest in our noble forest trees, causing them to be more fully appreciated, not only for their intrinsic worth, but because they are of the many blessings bestowed by the Creator upon this our country, then my object will be fully accomplished.

WOODSIDE, *March 30th*, 1866.

THE FOREST TREE CULTURIST.

CHAPTER I.

INTRODUCTION.

Every civilized nation feels more or less the need of an abundant supply of forest trees. Whether needed for timber to be used in the erection of houses, or in building ships, or for the more common but none the less important purpose of fuel, there is nothing that contributes more to the development of all the sources of national wealth and prosperity. America has felt this need the least; but the day is coming, if not already here, when her people will look back with regret to the time when forests were wantonly destroyed.

It is true there have been many cases where it was necessary to clear off the forest that the land might be cultivated and furnish the food necessary for the early settler; but it is well known that thousands of acres of valuable timber have been removed from land unfit for cultivation, the return from which would scarcely support the laborers who were employed in cutting and drawing it to the nearest market, or converting it into charcoal and ashes.

The land from which these forests were taken is now a silent waste, when, if the trees had remained upon it to this time, its increased value would have paid the interest on its original cost and taxes, and left a large surplus to the owner. Regrets over past follies will avail nothing unless they teach us to be wiser in the future.

In all of our large cities anxious inquiries are made for that indispensable article, timber. If we would extend commerce, ships and docks are needed, and for these more or less timber is required. The builders, the houseless and homeless, rich and poor, know and feel the need of it. Trees suitable for piles now command twenty to thirty dollars each. One of my neighbors not long since sold one hundred for three thousand dollars; ten years since half that amount would have been considered an exorbitant price. Firewood on the lines of our great railroads, miles away from our cities, sells for seven and eight dollars per cord; and if the demand continues to increase, soon it can not be had for double that amount. The demand increases, although coal and iron are persistent competitors; but the supply of wood decreases more rapidly. There is no reason why the supply should give out; there is land enough within reach of our great cities that lies uncultivated, or, what is more lamentable, unprofitably cultivated, that might be made to grow forests of good timber that would return to their owners a large profit on the investment.

I know many large land-owners who have been toiling for the past thirty years to lay up something to keep them in their old age and leave a balance to their children. They have worn themselves out as well as their land, and that something for which they have so arduously labored has not been obtained, and their children are likely to inherit a poor, worn-out farm instead of that competency which their father expected to have left them. Suppose these men had left one half their farms covered with the original forest, or if it was already cleared when they came into possession they had planted one half with forest trees, and then expended all their labor upon the other half, they would have produced better crops and with more profit; one half of their farm would have been rich, and the other half covered with a forest that would be a fortune worth inheriting.

Thousands of men are toiling this day to lay up wealth for their children, when if they would invest a small amount in land and then plant a few acres of our best forest trees, their money would grow into a fortune by the time their children had grown into manhood. To some this may appear visionary; but the writer has lived long enough to see trees grow from saplings that would hardly bear his weight at ten years old, up to great trees two feet in diameter, and he has scarcely passed the half-way house of three-score and ten.

In many portions of our country we need forests, not only for supplying us with timber, but for protection against winds and hurricanes. The farmer's grain is often prostrated by winds that never reached his fields until these protecting forests were destroyed. Fruit-growers are seeking the best means of shelter for their orchards, and a remedy for that dry atmosphere which sweeps through their gardens, shriveling up their finest specimens, checking, if not entirely annihilating, their ardor for fruit-growing.

The little stream that formerly came singing and dancing down from the great wood on the hill is now seen only for a few weeks in the early spring and fall, and then there is nothing left but its dry pebbly track. Is it not time we began to retrace our steps and again cover some of our now barren hillsides and many of our valleys with those trees which were not only an ornament and blessing to our land, but would now be a source of incalculable wealth?

The great West, with its wide-reaching treeless prairies, feels the need of forests even more than we do in the Atlantic States. The farmer on the prairies needs a shelter from the winds, the value of which no one but those who have experienced the want can appreciate. In no way can such a protection be provided better or cheaper than by a belt of trees. Then the convenience of having timber near at hand for building fences, stakes for vines, trees, and a thousand little necessities for which wood is indispensable.

A farmer who has provided a belt of trees around his farm has protected his fields from winds, and his grain will remain standing until ready to harvest. His fruit remains on the trees until ripe; and in a great measure his buildings are safe against those fearful hurricanes which frequently rush with such destructive force across those level plains. If people will persist in residing on those prairies, they certainly ought to be protected, but they should learn how to do it themselves, and not expect that Nature will rear it merely for the asking, without putting forth an effort on their part.

I have a vivid recollection of spending several years near those grand old prairies where the wind went and came without hindrance. One afternoon on coming home I found my house unroofed, and the place where a greenhouse stood in the morning swept clean, not a flower-pot, brick, or piece of glass left to show that I ever possessed a conservatory of fine plants. I can call to mind several instances of like character, each of which leads me to think that a *strong* protection is often required to enable the settler in the West to *keep* his foothold after he has obtained one.

The question is, *How* shall protection be the most readily provided?—how shall we get the trees we need? My only answer is, *Grow them!* This will require time and expense, most certainly—and what blessing does not? It takes time to get wealth, unless you are so fortunate, or unfortunate, as the case may be, as to have it given you; if so, it probably required time for the giver to obtain it. The great and important truth which I wish could be impressed upon the mind of every land-owner in America is, if you want improvements, *begin*, yes, begin them now! Do not put it off because you have no time to attend to it at present, nor because it will take so many years, and a little outlay at the start. You may say, "I can not wait so long." Who asks you to wait? Time moves in spite of you. Plant the seeds to-day, and while you are making up your mind whether you will wait a few years for them or not, the trees will be growing.

How often do we meet men with abundance of means who will tell you they would like to have a few trees here or there, a vineyard, or orchard, or a grove, and you propose that they should immediately commence planting;

the almost invariable answer will be, "I don't care for the expense, but I can't wait so long." I can count many such men among my acquaintances who have made the same excuse for the last ten or fifteen years, and they have not commenced that grove or vineyard yet, and done very little toward the orchard.

There are men, however, with whom to think and to act are near relatives, and a letter which I lately received from one who is a past octogenarian calls to mind a circumstance which happened several years ago; it also illustrates the fact, that there is never a period in life in which a man may not do some good to somebody by planting trees, and often he will gather the blessing himself, although he little expects it. When I was in my fourteenth year, a gray-haired uncle of sixty, who had just purchased a new farm, requested me to pull up some of the young trees which were growing in masses in my father's garden, and put them on a load of goods which were going to his place. With the assistance of my father I did so, tying the bundle to the body of the wagon, as there was no room on the load. I well remember the remark of my father at the time: "Uncle John, you are rather old to think of growing an orchard." "Never mind," replied my old uncle, "it is certainly not too late for me to try." That uncle still lives, and has been enjoying the fruit of those trees for many years. It is well that we can not all be sure of living to such a venerable age, for in that case I fear we would never begin, as "Time enough" would become the motto, instead of, as now, "No time."

The period has now arrived when this subject of growing

forest trees requires not only agitation but action. Our numerous agricultural societies should lend their aid by giving premiums for the best endeavors of individuals. Let there be lectures upon the subject, not by the city or village minister, lawyer, or editor, unless they know something about it *practically*, but by some of the plain men of the country who have no other title than Professor of Farming. These lectures should be delivered in a practical manner; not from some velvet-cushioned rostrum, but from an old log or stump of a tree in some forest or grove. In such a place the speaker can address his audience in an atmosphere filled with his subject, with examples above and around him. Here he can cut, hew, and prune to illustrate his theme without throwing the janitor of the building into hysterics through fear that a whittling might fall on the carpet.

In Europe they have arboricultural societies which have not only done much toward disseminating a correct knowledge of forest trees, but through whose influence thousands of acres of trees have been reared. There is no reason why such societies should not exist in this country; their usefulness, if rightly conducted, must be apparent to every casual observer.

There is no country on the globe that possesses such a numerous variety of valuable forest trees as America. Every article of usefulness of which wood is a part shows it; and if there is one branch of mechanics in which we excel more than in another, it is in our agricultural implements; and who does not know that one of their great points of excellence is the wood used in their construction?

The farmer is certainly more interested in these implements than any one else, and it devolves upon him to see to it that the requisite quantity and quality are supplied.

To one who has traveled through some of the great forests of the North and Northwest, it may seem unnecessary for Americans to ever attempt the cultivation of forest trees. But when we ask ourselves how these great forests can be transported to those regions where they are needed, the question assumes another phase, and we soon learn that transporting timber, especially by land, is a very laborious and expensive business. Even where railroads have penetrated regions abundantly supplied, we soon find that all along its track timber soon becomes scarce. For every railroad in the country requires a continued forest from one end to the other of its line to supply it with ties, fuel, and lumber for building their cars. Cars are continually wearing out, the ties are rotting, and the time is not far distant when these great monopolies will find that it would have been cheaper for them to have grown their own timber than to have depended on others to supply them. How simple it would be for the railroad companies to have a few acres of forest trees every few miles all along and contiguous to the line! Yet the farmers along these roads remember that timber will always be needed; and it is not always economy to cultivate with grain every piece of land from which you have taken the trees. Better let the sprouts grow, and the young seedlings which always show themselves soon after the large trees are cut away. A little thinning out of the least valuable kinds, and an occasional pruning of those left, will often prove to be a better plan and a much more profitable one than to clear off and plow up the soil.

If a particular kind of timber is wanted, then those trees should be left in preference to others. How few there are who have ever made a calculation of the value of an acre of White Oak, Hickory, Chestnut, or White Ash! As we find these in our native forests, they are mixed with other trees, often with those that are comparatively worthless. But suppose we have an acre purely of one kind, and that of the most valuable. What kind is most valuable must be ascertained by the grower himself, for it will depend upon his location, and which is in the greatest demand in his nearest market. Suppose we take Hickory, which is always in demand, when young, for hoop-poles, as it becomes larger for other purposes. There are other kinds equally as valuable and of more rapid growth. Now the young one or two year old plants, or even the nuts, may be put in rows four feet apart, and the plants one foot apart in the row; this will give 10,890 to the acre. At this distance they can be allowed to remain until they are six to eight feet high and one or two inches in diameter. They should reach this size in five to eight years, according to the soil and the care they receive. Then they should be thinned, by taking out every alternate tree; this should be done by cutting them off near the ground. We therefore take out 5,445 trees suitable for hoop-poles. Their value will of course depend upon the market, but we will say four cents each, or $40 per 1,000, which would be a low price in New York; this would give $217 80 (two hundred and seventeen dollars and eighty cents) as the return for the acre's first crop. In three or four years they will need thinning again, and we take out, as before, one half, or 2,722; these will, of course, be much larger; and if they will reach ten feet, and are of good thickness, they will readily bring ten cents each, or $272 20 for the second crop. In a few years more they will require thinning again, and each time the trees, being larger, will bring an increased price. But we are not by this means exhausting our stock—far from it, for those we cut off at first have been producing sprouts which have grown much more rapidly than the originals; and if a little care has been given them so that they shall not grow so thickly as to be injured thereby, we can begin to cut small hoop-poles from the sprouts of the first cutting before we have cut our third or fourth thinnings of the first crop; consequently we have a perpetual crop, which requires no cultivation after the first few years. As soon as the leaves become numerous enough to shade the ground, no weeds will grow among them, and the annual crop of leaves that fall will keep the soil rich and moist. The time to cut trees which it is desirous to have produce sprouts, is in winter or very early spring; if cut in summer, it is likely to kill the roots.

The same plan may be followed with many other varieties of trees that are valuable when young. Whether it will pay to grow such trees or not will depend entirely upon the location, market, etc., but there are few sections of our country in which such plantations would not be a very profitable investment.

Plantations of trees may be made in the form of belts

of a few feet or rods in width around the farm; and while they afford shelter and protection they will also become a source of revenue and profit. It is always best to plant the young trees near together at first, and then thin out as they grow. These annual thinnings, even where the object is to allow the main crop to grow to a large size, will more than pay for all the care and cost of the whole.

CHAPTER II.

PROPAGATION.

THERE is no occasion for a very scientific or elaborate description of the different methods employed in propagation of forest trees being given in a simple treatise like this. That they may be propagated in various ways is true, but the man who desires to grow only the native or more common exotic forest trees has no occasion to study the mysteries of horticultural science. I am well aware that it has been generally supposed among the farmers that it was only nurserymen that were able to grow such trees successfully; but this is an error; or, at least, if they do succeed better than others, it is only because they have given more attention to the subject; as it does not require any more skill to grow an acre of our common forest trees than it does to grow an acre of cabbage or corn. They require no better preparation of soil or any better after-culture than a majority of our ordinary farm crops.

The cost of producing seedling trees is also much less than those unacquainted with the subject would suppose. Having grown many thousands, I think that a fair estimate of cost at one year old, taking one variety with another, will not exceed two dollars per thousand. This estimate includes the cost of seed, preparing soil, hoeing, weeding, etc., for one season. The cost will certainly depend somewhat upon the price paid for seed, for there are some kinds of the more rare native trees, such as the Magnolia, Cladrastis, etc., the seeds of which would cost nearly the amount named. My estimate refers mainly to the different varieties of Maple, Ash, Oak, Tulip, Spruce, and similar kinds, the seeds of which are always to be had very cheap. The larger nut-bearing trees, such as Chestnut, Walnut, Hickory, Butternut, etc., would cost a trifle more, as they are always in demand for other purposes than for growing trees. Besides being more bulky, the cost of transportation is proportionably greater. Where the seeds can be had near at hand, the cost per thousand ought not to be more than the sum named. I do not wish to estimate the cost too low, but having grown and sold many thousands of such trees, I feel qualified to name a price, because it is derived from actual experience. No one must expect to *buy* trees at two dollars per thousand, because those who grow them for sale expect, and have a right to demand, a profit. Every one who wants forest trees in large quantities should learn how to grow them upon their own land, then they will have them near at hand when wanted, and can transplant them at their leisure. All of our most valuable forest trees are readily grown from seed, there being only a few kinds—and most of these are of an inferior quality—which are more easily grown from cuttings.

I will give my own method of growing the different varieties, although it may or may not accord with the practice of others; the results, however, have always been satisfactory.

SEED-BED.

For nearly all of the hardy deciduous trees (*i. e.*, those that lose their leaves in the autumn), an open field is a good situation for a seed-bed. The soil should be deep, mellow, and rich; if not so, make it so by frequent plowing and thoroughly pulverizing with the harrow. If not rich, apply a good liberal dressing of any old well-decomposed manure. Good barn-yard is good enough if old; muck, rotted sods, or leaf mold from the woods will answer every purpose. If none of these are at hand, then bone-dust or ashes may be used; a ton to the acre will not be too much of the latter, or from fifty to one hundred two-horse loads of the muck and leaf mold, and half that quantity of manure. Double this amount would be still better, unless your soil is good at the start. Mix these applications thoroughly with the soil, and harrow all down smooth and level, and your seed-bed is ready. Now draw a line

Fig. 1.

across one side of the plot, and with a hoe make a shallow trench from a half to one inch deep, according to the size of the seeds to be sown. (Fig. 1 shows a wide seed drill or trench when ready for the seeds.) Make the trench about one foot wide; scatter the seeds over the bottom, but not too thickly, say one to two inches apart, and then draw the soil back and cover the seeds as evenly as possible. These seed-beds or wide drills should be four feet apart if a cultivator is to be used among them; if not, and only the hoe or spading-fork is to be employed in cultivation, then two feet will be sufficient. All that will now be required is to keep the soil loose between the rows, and keep them clear of weeds, keeping in mind that, like other crops, better the care, the better results. The smaller the seeds the less they should be covered, although some small seeds will bear covering much deeper than some large ones. Maple, Elm, Oak, Beech, Tulip, etc., not more than a half inch, while Hickory, Chestnut, and Black Walnut about one inch. I sometimes sow the coarser seeds in single drills, having only one row instead of the wide bed; in this case the corner of the hoe is only used to make the trench.

Where there is no scarcity of land, the single drill is in some respects preferable, as it is less trouble in weeding, and the plants will usually grow larger than when sown more thickly. Still, the wide drill has its advantages, for more plants can be grown on an acre; besides, the plants shade one another, and thereby are not quite so liable to be burned by the sun, as in single drills. There are, however, but few kinds that are liable to be damaged by burning, even in our hottest weather, and these should be grown in a half shady position. Some varieties are benefited by being partially shaded when they first appear above ground, also by being protected from the cold the first winter, consequently it is best to sow the seeds of these in small beds, say four feet wide and as long as required. Around these beds set up boards a foot or more in width, fastening them with stakes or by nailing them together at the corners, and by placing cross-bars every four feet along their length. The soil in these beds should be made fine and rich, and raked level before the seeds are sown. Sow in drills six inches apart, or broad-cast, and rake in. After sowing, put on the screen, which may be of coarse matting, or evergreen boughs, or, what is better, one made with laths. These lath screens should be long enough to lie cross-wise of the frames, and about three or

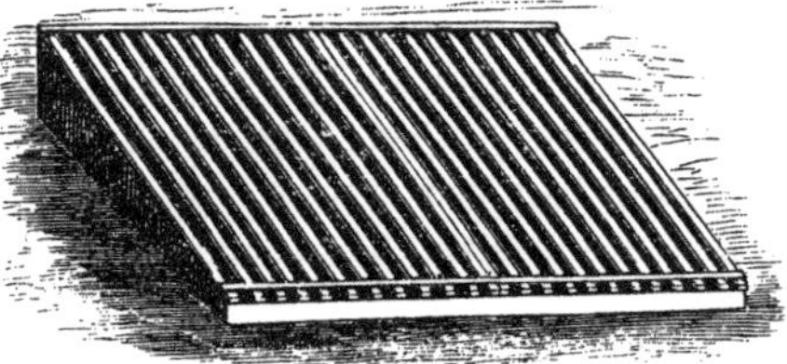

Fig. 2.

four feet wide. (Fig. 2 shows an inclosed seed-bed covered with a lath screen.) If the seed-bed is not over four feet wide, one length of common lath will cover it cross-wise; then by nailing a narrow strip of board across the ends of the lath, your frame screen will be complete. The laths should be placed one to two inches apart; this will allow plenty of light to reach the soil, but not enough to injure the plants; it will also allow the rain to find access to the beds. These lath screens are the most convenient, cost but little, and will last a long time if placed under cover when not in use. The sun reaches every part of the bed through the screens in the course of the day, but does not remain long enough on any particular spot to cause injury. A board fence or hedge running east and west will often answer very well for a screen for the more delicate varieties which require it; on the north side of these make the bed, and only so wide as will be shaded in the middle of the day.

Most of the evergreens require a little protection from the sun when they first come up. There are also some of our deciduous trees which are rather tender and often burn off when they first appear above ground. The Mountain Ash, Larch, Taxodium, and some others, often fail entirely for the want of a little protection at this time. No general rule will apply to all, nor can there be any specific rule which will apply to each and every section of the country; as soil and climate vary, so must practice. It is better to be careful than careless, therefore it is better to use a preventive than risk a failure. When I come to speak of the different varieties, I shall indicate kinds which are better sown in shady situations than in open ground. It may not always be necessary, but is certainly the safest. Seeds sown in these beds with screens should not be covered too deep, and the best way to do it is with a sieve, whether in drills or otherwise.

The best soil for covering is fine leaf mold, so well rotted that it will pass readily through a sieve with one eighth of an inch meshes. It will often be necessary to water these seed-beds, especially when the small and delicate varieties are sown, as such must not be covered more than one fourth of an inch deep; and unless the surface of the soil is kept moist, they will very likely fail to come up. A very light sprinkling every day in dry weather is what they require, not a drenching to-day and no more for a week or two. Keep the soil moist, but not wet.

When the plants first come up, and have formed but few leaves, is the time the most care must be used in watering, and no more should be applied than they actually require to keep them from suffering for the want of it. Too much moisture at this time, especially if the weather is very warm, will cause them to damp off, or, in other words, rot off. Remove the screens in cloudy weather that the plants may get plenty of air, for our object just at this time is to harden the plants or make their stems firm and woody, not by drying them, but by a healthy growth. So soon as they are from two to six inches in height (according to the varieties), very little care is required. If the weather should be very dry, give them water; but the sprinklings may be dispensed with, and a good soaking be given instead, but only occasionally or when the plants really need it. For evergreens, the screens may be kept on the beds most of the summer, but remove toward fall so that the plants may be thoroughly ripened. At the approach of winter, or so soon as the ground begins to freeze, put on the screens or lay strips across the top of the frames, and on these place straw, hay, cornstalks, evergreen boughs, or any such material that may be at hand. It is not expected that the frost will be entirely excluded, nor would it be advisable to do so, for there would be danger of smothering the plants. The covering is merely to prevent the frequent freezing and thawing of the ground and heaving out the plants.

TIME FOR SOWING SEEDS.

There can be no specified time given for sowing all kinds of tree seeds, but for a general rule, very soon after they ripen is the best. It is certainly not always convenient to do so, nor is it always necessary, but with some kinds a delay of a few weeks is almost certain to result in a complete failure. Some kinds of seeds retain their vitality for years, while others for only a few months at most.

The want of specific knowledge upon this point has been the cause of many failures, and will probably continue to be so until more general information is disseminated. To more fully illustrate this point, I will suppose a case. Mr. B., a farmer at the West, wishes to grow a quantity of the different kinds of maples, and he writes to some Eastern seedsman ordering two bushels of each of the following kinds: Sugar Maple, Norway Maple, Red Maple, Silver Maple, sending his order in the fall, knowing that at that time most trees ripen their seeds. But for once he has made a mistake; and if he has sent his order to an honest and intelligent seedsman, he will fill one half of Mr. B.'s order, and write him why he does not send him all the seeds ordered. But if he has sent his order to one who is not posted up in the matter, or who values money more than honesty, he will fill the order complete, and the result will be that the seeds of the first two kinds will grow, and the others not.

The Red and Silver Maple ripen their seeds in spring or early summer, about the first to the middle of June in this vicinity, and they retain their vitality for only a few weeks. If sowed so soon as ripe, they will come up in a few days, and make a growth of one to three feet by the time the Sugar and Norway Maple seeds are ripe in autumn.

If Mr. B. had been aware of this fact, he would have sent his order for them early in spring, and have directed that they should be forwarded to him in bags, or, what is better, baskets, but not in close boxes, for when excluded from the air, or closely packed together, they will heat, and soon be destroyed. These two varieties of maples are among the few forest tree seeds that absolutely demand immediate planting, and then they grow very readily.

CHAPTER III

PRESERVING SEEDS.

As before remarked, some kinds of seeds retain their vitality for a long time, and others only for a short period. Those seeds that have a firm, horn-like covering, like the Locust, Virgilia, etc., generally retain their vitality the longest, while the seeds of the Maple, Elm, and similar trees that have a very porous covering, are comparatively short-lived. The size of the seed is no indication of its vitality; the largest may perish much sooner than the very smallest.

The Black Walnut, Horse Chestnut, and Butternut will seldom if ever grow after the first season, while the Virgilia and Locust, which are quite small, will germinate after having been kept for a dozen years. The vitality of all seeds may be retained for a much longer time than was evidently intended by Nature, if they are placed under the proper conditions. A cool, dry, and equal temperature appears to be the best adapted for the preservation of all seeds. The humidity of the atmosphere has also much to do in enabling them to retain their vitality, for while a warm, moist one is just suited to growth, it hastens the death of the seeds. For when the germinating powers of the seed have once been excited into growth, it can not be checked without injuring, if not wholly destroying, its vitality. A warm, dry atmosphere evaporates the moisture, causing them to shrivel, and thus destroys them.

Some seeds, as the Chestnut, contain such a large amount of albuminous matter that it is quite difficult to keep the temperature and humidity of the atmosphere just in the right state for their preservation. All such seeds should be placed in the ground, or on it, soon after they are ripe, and covered with leaves or some similar material, following Nature's method, as they receive there the proper degree of warmth and moisture requisite to their preservation, better than in any other situation.

GATHERING AND TRANSPORTING SEEDS.

Seeds should always be gathered in dry weather, and those kinds which are inclosed in an outer covering, like the Butternut, should be spread out in an airy situation until they are quite dry before being packed for transportation. It is also advisable to dry all tree seeds a little, but it must be varied according to the size and natural amount of moisture they contain. Those that possess a large amount either in their covering or in the seed proper are liable to heat if packed in close air-tight boxes. Baskets and bags, or boxes with small holes bored in them, should be used for the purpose, especially if the seeds are to remain in them for several days. Sheets of paper, or layers of dry moss, may be placed between the layers of seeds to absorb the moisture, when necessary to pack the seeds before they are sufficiently dry. These remarks only apply to the larger seeds and those that naturally contain considerable moisture at the time of gathering.

The smaller seeds as well as larger ones that are inclosed in a dry covering, such as the Alder, Spruce, and Pine among the smaller, and Beech and Hickory among the larger, may be transported in bags, barrels, or tight boxes; all that is necessary is to keep them dry while on transit.

WHERE TO OBTAIN SEED.

Where shall we get our seeds? is a question that admits of only a very general answer. It is apparent to all, that where the trees grow, there will the seeds be found most abundant.

The sections of country where the different trees most abound will be pointed out in the following pages. If in those sections there are any persons who gather seeds for sale, whose address you can obtain, they will be glad to furnish you, otherwise you may have some acquaintance there who will take the trouble to gather them for you; or, this failing, you could write to a postmaster in the vicinity stating your desire, and asking him to aid you by giving you the address of some one who would be likely to furnish them, inclosing a prepaid envelope for the answer. Our country postmasters are generally accommodating men, and if you do not ask them to write a long letter and pay the postage themselves, on business which wholly benefits yourself, you will find them ready to do a favor even to a stranger. When you get the address of the person, write him stating in a few words what you desire; and if he can not get the seeds for you, ask him if he can refer you to some one who can (always inclosing a postage stamp for reply). There are many ways in which a correspondence may be brought about between farmers, in different parts of the country, which would result in advantage to both parties. Seeds could be exchanged, and information upon various subjects given and received. If farmers would write and study more and work less, they would get rich sooner, live longer, and be more happy.

When the seeds wanted can not be procured in this way, then write to some seedsman for them, always sending in your order early; never wait until it is time to sow the seeds before ordering them. Few seedsmen save any more than they are likely to sell, not wishing to incur the expense of having a large quantity gathered to supply an uncertain demand.

And here let me say to those who are about ordering seeds: You will not only be more certain of getting what you want, but you will accommodate the seedsman by sending your order a month—yes, six months—before you require them. It is not necessary that you should send the full amount of cost with the order, but you should send a small sum, unless you are personally known to the one to whom you send your order. If you wish to buy fifty or one hundred dollars' worth, send five or ten dollars along with the order, as this will show that you are in earnest and intend to buy what you have asked for, and your order will be put on the order-book. If you merely write saying that at some future time you will want such articles, ten to one your letter goes into the waste-basket and no notice taken of it. Perhaps Mr. Seedsman has ten just such letters from different parties the same day yours reached him, and he knows from past experience that probably not more than one out of the ten will buy the seeds about which they have written to inquire.

There has been for many years quite a demand for American forest tree seeds in Europe, and a few of our seedsmen have made a specialty of gathering them. There is an abundant supply, and our seedsmen possess the facility and energy to meet the demand for any amount that may be required. But do send in your orders *early*.

CHAPTER IV.

GROWING FROM CUTTINGS.

THERE are a few kinds of trees that are more readily grown from cuttings than from seeds, among which are the different species of Willow, Poplar, Buttonwood, etc. Sometimes seeds of other kinds can not be obtained as readily as cuttings; and when they are of varieties which can be easily propagated in this manner, then it will be desirable to do so.* When cuttings are to be grown in the open ground, it is best to cut them in the fall, so soon as they have cast their leaves, and heel them in, away from the frost, until spring.

The safest place to keep cuttings during winter is in some dry place in the open ground, and either have them tied in small convenient bundles or laid in trenches, after which cover so deep that they will not freeze.

The length of the cutting will depend somewhat upon the kind, but from six to twelve inches is usually the most convenient. If in bundles, they should be tied with tough willow, tarred twine, or some similar material, as ordinary hemp or cotton twine may become rotten before the

* The scientific horticulturist who has propagating-houses at command, experiences no great difficulty in multiplying those varieties of which he can not obtain seeds, or grow from ripe wood cuttings, by using the green growing wood in summer ; but such a process belongs to him alone, and not to the common farmer, for whom this work is especially written.

cuttings are wanted for planting. In spring, so soon as the weather is suitable, take out the cuttings and plant them in trenches made with a plow or spade, placing them two or three inches apart in the row, and the rows from two to four feet apart, according to the manner in which they are to be cultivated. The cuttings should be placed nearly their whole length in the ground, and in an upright position, leaving only an inch or two above the surface. Press the soil firmly around them, and give the same care as for seedlings, with a similar soil and situation.

These remarks apply only to deciduous trees, and are general in their character. Specific directions as to whether the cuttings are to be made of young or old wood, will be noticed in another place. In making the cuttings, it is always best to cut just below a bud, and square across instead of sloping, although it will make but little difference except with those kinds which have a large pith; with such kinds there is danger of too much water entering the lower part of the cutting and causing it to decay before it can take root. But if cut off just at the base of a bud, this is prevented, as at this point there is usually a cross section of wood entirely closing the space occupied by the pith in other portions of the stem.

Some kinds of evergreen trees may also be readily propagated by cuttings. This is only advisable when seeds can not be obtained, or when it is desirable to multiply some particular variety upon whose seeds, if they were to be obtained, there could be no certainty of getting plants like the parent. The Arborvitæs, Junipers, Yews, etc., are often successfully propagated without artificial heat.

The cuttings of these are taken off early in the fall and placed in frames similar to the one described for seeds.

Cuttings are made of the ends of the branches, and mainly of the present season's growth, with perhaps a little of the two-year-old wood attached. They should be three or four inches in length, and the leaves of the lower half cut away; cut off the lower end smooth and square

Fig. 3.

across the stem, being careful not to crush the wood. Fig. 3 shows a cutting of Arborvitæ prepared for planting. Place these in the soil about one half their length, and in rows six inches apart; press the earth firmly about them; give water sufficient to settle the soil; they should be covered then, or so soon as the ground begins to freeze, and remain undisturbed until spring. If glazed frames can be put over them, and kept partially shaded until covered for winter, it will facilitate the production of roots. They should be kept shaded until well rooted; for if the sun is allowed to come fully upon them, it will excite the leaves into growth; and if no roots have been previously formed, no permanent growth can take place, and the cuttings die. Our object is to obtain roots first, afterward growth of top.

It is well known that roots will form at a much lower temperature than leaves; and we take advantage of this fact by placing the cuttings in the frames, where they will remain so cool that there will be no growth of leaves, while the lower portion, which is underground, is in a position warm enough for the production of roots.

Most of the evergreens emit roots very slowly from ripe wood cuttings. But if the frames are comparatively warm during winter (as they may be easily made by being well banked and covered), small roots will be produced by the time warm weather approaches in spring. The cuttings should remain in the frames during the first summer, and be treated as though they were seedlings, being protected in winter. Cuttings of the young growing wood in summer can also be very readily grown in a hot-bed, but this requires more care than with ripe wood, and very few would succeed if they attempted it, except those who fully understand the management of hot-beds.

As I propose to give only the most simple and easiest modes of multiplying our forest trees, I will omit further particulars upon propagating them by cuttings.

CHAPTER V.

BUDDING, GRAFTING, ETC.

OTHER methods of propagating than those already given will seldom be employed or are necessary for those who grow trees for shelter or timber. There will, however, sometimes cases occur when it would be quite advantageous even for the common farmer to propagate certain trees by other methods instead of cuttings and seeds. Trees will often vary considerably when grown from seeds. Maple seeds will certainly produce Maple trees; still, occasionally, a seedling will be found that is quite distinct from all the others; and if it should possess some peculiar and striking characteristic which it would be desirable to perpetuate, then we must have recourse to some other method of propagating it than that of seeds, because it would take a long time for the new variety to grow to a bearing size; besides, its seeds would be just as likely to vary, and even more so than the seeds from which it was grown.

When trees have once shown any considerable variation from the original type, and the natural or fixed characters have changed, they are likely to sport more widely in the future generations than in the first one. This principle is so well known among horticulturists, that they always strive, when operating with a distinct species, to so influence it that its seedlings will be different from the parent plant.

A variation is also often effected by moving a plant from its native country or soil to another; and when this change has once taken place, and the foundation of generation has been broken up, then variations become as common and apparently as natural as the fixed character was in the beginning. All, or nearly all, of our cultivated fruits and flowers are the results of the breaking up of the natural or original types from which the different species were derived. Knowing this, we should always watch for variations, and when discovered, preserve them with great care.

When trees assume any particular form or character from the natural one, they are said to *sport*, and thus we have as sports of the Maple the striped-leaved, purple-leaved, etc. In nearly every species of ornamental trees we have such sports, and many of them are very beautiful, affording a most pleasing variety of color and form of foliage, and perhaps all were derived from a single species, though often several have contributed one or more of the number.

Variations that possess any particular merit or value are not common, still they are sufficiently so to warrant us to be on the look-out for them, especially when a large number of seedlings are grown. It will always be worth while for the grower to carefully look over his seedlings, and if he should discover any one or more that show any peculiar form or color of foliage, or any particular habit of growth different from the mass, let them be marked, and at the proper time taken up and planted by themselves, where their future development may be carefully observed. We have a fine pyramidal-growing Maple; but a weeping one would be still more desirable. Such a tree will be produced, but when, or by whom, the future will unfold.

When a really fine sport or variety has been produced, no time should be lost in multiplying it, as there is always danger of losing the original; and if this should occur, then all is lost, unless we have propagated others from it. Now there are several ways of propagating such trees, but I shall mention only three, viz., Layering, Budding, and Grafting.

LAYERING.

This mode of propagating is almost as natural as that of seeds, as we see many plants that increase in this manner. Whenever the branches come in contact with the earth they emit roots; these layers throw up shoots which form plants, trees, or shrubs, and their branches again bending to the ground repeat the process, and so on indefinitely. But with those trees of which we shall treat in the following pages, very few, if any, would increase in this manner unless assisted or compelled to do so. The principle, or, more properly, the theory, of Layering may be explained as follows:

A tree absorbs plant-food through its roots (this being always in the liquid form); it is then carried up through the alburnum (or what is commonly called the sap-wood) to the buds and leaves; it is there assimilated chiefly by the leaves, and the more volatile portions are given off; it then returns downward through the inner bark, and between it and the wood depositing a thin layer of alburnous matter, which becomes soon after fully formed wood. Now this material is deposited from the ends of the branches to the ends of the lowest root, so that we see that branches and roots are formed of one and the same material; and if we wish to convert a branch into roots at any particular point, we have only to give it an opportunity of escaping into a congenial and natural element. Consequently, when we wish to make a branch produce roots so that it shall become capable of living independently of the parent plant, we bend it down and cover that portion on which we wish to produce roots, at the same time making an incision through the bark and into the wood, so as to arrest or cut off the downward flow of sap at that particular point. This cutting the branch is not always necessary with all kinds to insure the production of roots; still, it hastens the process, even with those that produce their roots most readily. But we must not cut so deeply as to prevent the upward flow, because we wish the branch to live and grow until it has produced sufficient roots to sup-

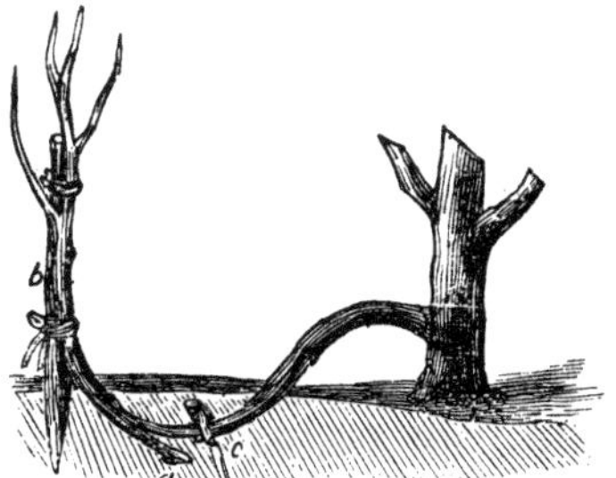

Fig. 4.

port itself. As a general rule, the branch may be cut half through, and on the under side, and if slightly split, it will be all the better. Fig. 4 shows a layer as it appears when buried in the soil. The incision is made in the branch before bending it down, and the knife inserted just below a bud, passing into the wood, and then an inch or more lengthwise, the branch forming what is termed a tongue—see fig. 4, *a*. A hooked peg is usually employed to hold the layer in its place, as it is important that it should be held firm, so that it may not be swayed about by the wind.

Layers may be made at almost any time, but they will root sooner if made in early or mid-summer than if made earlier or later. But as they should not be separated from the parent plant until the wood is ripe in the fall, or the leaves have fallen, if from deciduous trees, it is well to make them in spring as soon as the trees have put forth their leaves, so that they shall have sufficient time to become well rooted by fall.

Evergreen trees should be layered while the trees are in full growth, and not before or after. It will sometimes require two seasons for layers of some trees to become sufficiently rooted to be separated; it is therefore necessary to carefully examine those that emit roots tardily before separating them. Some kinds of trees will produce roots when layered without cutting the branch—in fact, all will in time; but the surest way is to expose the alburnum to the soil. Sometimes a part of a tree, or a small branch thereof, will vary from the original; when this occurs on a large tree, and where the branch can not be made to reach the ground, we must elevate the soil or some similar material to the part that we wish to propagate, unless it be a variety which can be readily propagated from cuttings, buds, or grafting.

Suppose a single branch of Beech should produce leaves that were pure silver-white (and I know of one that does), and we wish to obtain plants from it; as the Beech will not grow from cuttings, and is difficult to bud and graft (at least the novice would find it so), we desire to obtain a layer; now we have only to place a pot or box of soil near the branch so that we can layer it into the soil the same as we would if near the ground, after which it will be necessary to keep it moist to facilitate the produc-

Fig. 5.

tion of roots. Fig. 5 shows a branch layered in a pot that has had a piece taken from the side and the branch passed through it; this crevasse is closed by a piece of board or shingle placed on the inside of the pot; the pot is then filled with soil, and the branch is layered. It is well to surround the pot with moss, or several thicknesses of cloth, so that the wind will not dry the soil too quickly, as in that case it will require very frequent watering.

A box will answer every purpose as well as a pot; all

that is necessary is to make the incision in the branch before putting it in the earth, and then see that it does not become so dry that the roots can not grow.

BUDDING.

Budding consists in taking from one tree a bud, with a small piece of bark attached, and transferring it to another. The tree upon which it is placed is called the stock. The limits of this operation are not very well defined; but for all practical purposes it need not be extended beyond the members of the same genus; that is, Maples may be budded on Maples; and generally, the nearer related the species, the more successful the operation. But, like other rules in Horticulture, there are exceptions, and sometimes by budding a weak-growing kind on a strong-growing one, we make a decided improvement. Again, it must not be supposed that all the individuals of one genus can be worked indiscriminately one upon another; for the Black Mazzard Cherry of Europe and the Wild Black Cherry of America are classed by our best botanists as belonging to one genus, still neither will grow upon the other. Many similar instances might be named; in fact, to minutely describe all the variations which occur, or the different methods employed to reach the same results, would fill a volume by itself.

Budding is usually performed in summer, just after the buds, or a portion of them, are fully developed on the young wood of the present season's growth. The stock into which the buds are to be inserted must also be in a similar condition, so that the bark will part readily from the wood, as the bud or the bark attached to it is to be inserted under the bark of the stock, and unless this can be done the operation will usually fail. We have to depend upon assimilated or true sap to form the junction between the bud and stock, the same as we did with the layers to produce roots, for the operations are analogous; only in budding, the alburnous matter forms a union with the same material in the stock, while in the layer it is emitted in the form of roots.

HOW PERFORMED.

In fig. 6, *a*, we have a bud which is to be transferred to the stock; a knife is inserted about one inch below it and passed upward, and brought out about a half inch above it, cutting out a piece of bark with a thin slice of wood, of

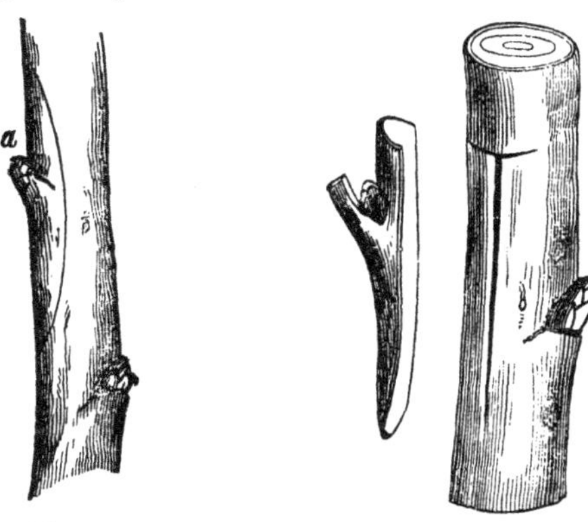

Fig. 6. Fig. 7.

a form as shown by the circular line in the figure. We now make a cut across the stock, cutting just through the bark, and then another longitudinally downward about an inch long, as shown in fig. 7; then insert the lower end of the bark containing the bud under the bark of the stock at the point where the incisions meet, and press it down to its place. If the bark of the stock is firm and does not part easily, the edges must be lifted slightly so as to allow the bud to pass under it freely. If the portion with the bud does not pass completely under, then cut off the bark at the upper end even with the cross cut in the stock so that it shall fit it smoothly. In fig. 7 a bud is shown taken out after the upper end has been cut off to fit. And on this is also shown a portion of a leaf stem as it is usually left. When buds are taken from the young wood, the leaves are cut off, leaving only about a half inch of the lower portion of the stem.

After the bud is inserted, it is then secured in its place by a ligature, which may be of bass bark, woolen yarn, soft twine, or some similar material. Fig. 8 shows a bud as it appears when tied in its place. The stock should not be over an inch in diameter, nor much less than one half inch, whether it be upon the main stem of a seedling or upon the branch of a large tree. After the bud has firmly united to the stock, which will usually be in two or three weeks, the ligature should be loosened, or removed entirely. The bud is not expected to push into growth until the next spring (nor is it desirable that it should, though it sometimes will), at which time the stock above the bud should be cut away and the bud allowed to grow undisturbed. If sprouts appear on the stock they should

Fig. 8.

be removed, so that all the strength may be given to the bud.

The implement with which this operation is performed is called a budding-knife, and they are made of different forms, but the one in common use in the larger nurseries in this vicinity is similar in form to the one shown in fig. 9. It is here shown of full size, and may be made expressly for the purpose; or any small knife with a thin blade of good material may have the end rounded, and will answer very well unless a large number of trees are to be budded, then it will be well to get knives made expressly for the purpose. The rounded end is used to lift the bark of the stock instead of using a thin ivory handle, as seen on old-time budding knives.

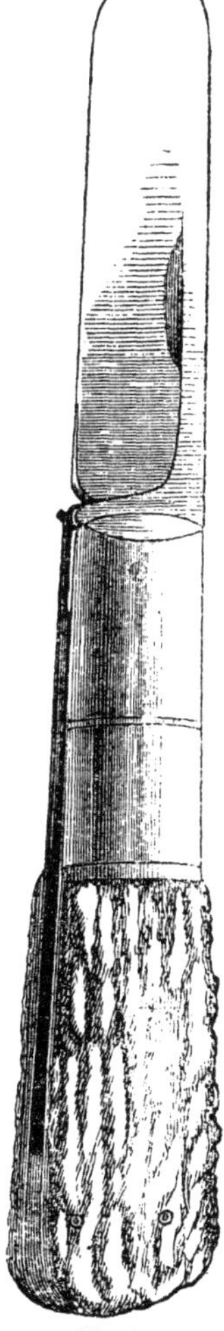
Fig. 9.

ANNULAR BUDDING.

This differs from the preceding in two particulars: first, the bud is not inserted under the bark of the stock, but is fitted to it. A ring of bark passing completely around the stem upon which is a bud, is taken from a branch, and a similar ring is cut from the stock, and the bud and bark are fitted into this and then carefully tied in its place. The branch from which the bud is taken, and the stock to which it is affixed, should be of nearly the same size. Fig. 10 shows a stock and the ring of bark, with bud ready to be clasped around it. Second, it differs from the other mode of budding because it may be performed as readily in spring, when the bark first begins to peel, as at any other time, and is just as certain at that time as in summer.

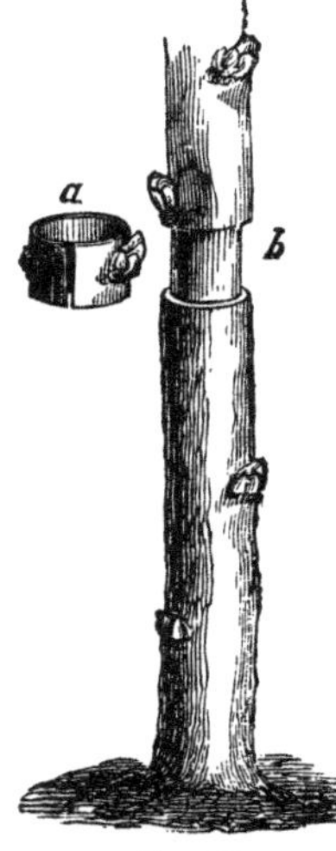

Fig. 10

The other modes of budding may also be performed in spring, but not with so much certainty of success as in summer. Annular budding is not a common practice, because it is too tedious; yet it is an excellent method of propagation where only a few trees are to be worked. Some of our forest trees, especially the Chestnut, are readily budded in this manner.

GRAFTING.

Grafting is a very common mode of propagating trees, and it should be — but is not — understood by every farmer in the land; for there is not one among them all who has not occasion to graft some fruit or forest tree every year of his life. Cleft grafting is the most common mode, and is chiefly employed when the stock is considerably larger than the graft. It is generally done in spring, just before the leaves push, or, in other words, just as the buds begin to swell, and is performed as follows.

The stock, whether it be a branch of a large tree or a young seedling of one or two inches in diameter, is cut off square across with a saw; it is then split with a chisel or knife, and the cleft kept open by a wedge until the graft (which is usually called a cion) is inserted; the cion is usually made from a young branch of the last year's growth, about three inches long, containing two or three buds. The lower end is made wedge-shape, the two sides being sloped about an inch and a half; it is then inserted in the cleft, care being taken that the outside of the wood of the cion and stock are just even, or, in other words, that the inside of the bark of each meets that of the other. The wedge employed to keep the cleft open is withdrawn when the cions are inserted. Two cions may be inserted in each stock, if it be more than an inch in diameter; but only one should be allowed to grow, always reserving the best, after it is known that both have united. Fig. 11 shows a stock cleft grafted, also a cion ready for insertion. After the cions have been fixed in place, the end of the stock and down the cleft should be covered with grafting-wax, to prevent the wind drying the exposed wood, as well as to exclude air and water and preventing a union taking place.

Fig. 11.

SPLICE GRAFTING.

This method is employed when the stock and cion are

nearly the same size, and is performed at the same time of year as the preceding. The stock is cut off with an upward slope, making the exposed wood perfectly smooth; a cion of two to four inches long is cut off with the same slope as the stock, and fitted to it, being careful to have the wood and bark on one side fit exactly. It would be better if both did, but this can not be done unless the cion and stock are of an exact size, which it would be difficult to always have. A small cleft or split may be made in the stock and cion about midway on the slope, forming a tongue on both; these are then inserted one into the other, which will hold the cion firmly in its place. Fig. 12 shows the operation better than words can describe it: *c*, the stock; *b*, cion; *a*, bud on cion, the union being formed by a tongued splice; *d* shows a cion without being tongued. The common splice without the tongue is the best for the coarse, brittle woods; but when it is fine-grained and tough, and cuts smooth, then the tongue can be employed with benefit. The junction between the stock and graft should be covered with waxed cloth wound around tightly, so that it shall hold it firmly in place.

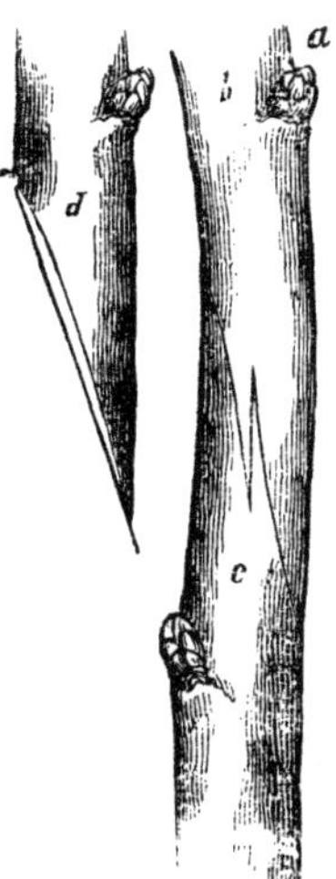

Fig. 12.

GRAFTING-WAX.

There are as many different recipes for making grafting-wax as there are modes of grafting, yet I have not learned that any of the new compositions are better than the old, consequently I will give the method of making that which a century has proven to be good. The ingredients are beeswax, resin, and tallow in the following proportions: one pound of taliow, two pounds of beeswax, and four pounds of resin melted together. If to be used in cool weather, add a little more tallow. If waxed cloth is wanted, take common muslin or calico and spread the wax on it when it is melted; or the cloth may be dipped in the wax when it is quite hot, so that but little will adhere. The wax or waxed cloth will remain good for years, and will always be found quite handy to cover the wounds of trees that may be accidentally made while working among them. A wound covered so soon as made will soon heal over, when, if exposed to the air, it may be the cause of disease that will eventually destroy the tree.

CHAPTER VI.

TRANSPLANTING.

MOST of our young seedling trees, as well as those from cuttings, will need transplanting after the first season's growth. But like all the other operations, it requires only ordinary judgment to determine this point. If the young trees have grown vigorously, and are likely to be too much crowded before another season's growth is over, then they should be taken up and given more room. But if they have made only a moderate growth, and are not standing too thickly, they may remain in the seed-bed another year.

Another point must also be settled by the grower, and that is, whether it is better to take up the young plants in the fall and heel them in for protection in winter, or let them remain in the bed. If the ground is of a kind that usually heaves (as it is termed) in winter, thereby endangering the young plants, then it would be better to take all the plants up in the fall.

Some kinds, like the Maple and Elm, make an abundance of fibrous roots the first year, and are in no danger of being thrown out even upon wet soil; while some others, like the Oak and Hickory, make one long, carrot-like root the first year with few small roots, and are very liable to be thrown out unless the soil is very dry and porous. I have now particular reference to young seedling deciduous trees. When they become larger, say four to six years old, the fall is then the preferable time to transplant, as the ground becomes settled about the roots during winter, and wounds upon them will form rootlets much earlier in the spring than if transplanting is delayed until that time. But fall planting is usually done too late, and the ground does not get well settled around the roots before it freezes. If done at all at this season, it should be just so soon as the leaves fall or have ceased acting on the plant. In sections of the country where the fall of the leaf is immediately followed by cold freezing weather, transplanting large trees should be deferred to early spring. North of the latitude of New York city I would not advise planting any yearling or two-year-old trees in the fall, as the roots of such are not unusually large or numerous enough to hold them firmly, and they are more likely to be injured by the frost than if planted in the spring, when they will have time to become well rooted before being subjected to cold weather. But when young trees are to be transplanted from seed or cutting bed, they should be taken up in the fall and fully prepared for planting in spring.

This preparation consists mainly in cutting off the tap-root and all the side branches. Fig. 13 shows a one-year seedling Black Walnut, the cross line, *c*, indicating the point where it should be cut off. One third to two thirds of the length of the tap-root should be cut away, as it facilitates the emission of side roots when planted again. These side or lateral roots spread through the soil, giving the tree a wider range for obtaining food than if the

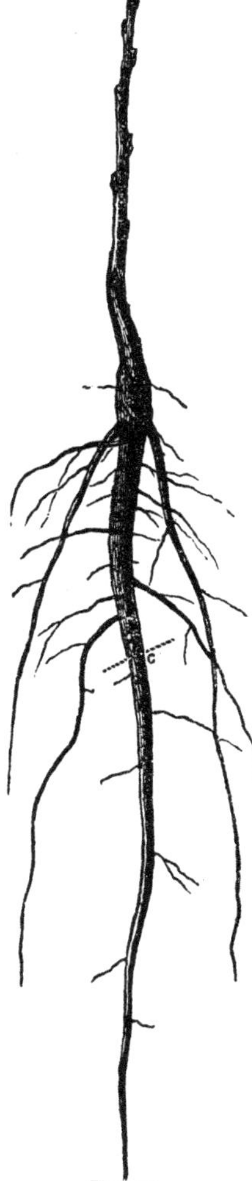

Fig. 13.

growth of the tap-root was encouraged. Thus by changing the habit of the plant we increase its growth.

Seedling trees of one season's growth seldom have many side branches; but when there are any, it is best to cut them entirely away, preserving only the one main stem. The main shoot should not be disturbed, except in some particular cases that may occur, as we wish to get a straight stem at the start, no matter whether we wish to head it back in after years or not. Long and elaborate essays upon the cutting off the tap-root are to be found in nearly all of our larger works on Horticulture, some in favor of, and others denouncing, the practice with all the theory at command. I believe it to be best to cut them off, as it renders the young tree more convenient to plant, besides placing it in a position most favorable to its future growth.

When we allow the plants to remain in the seed-beds two years, there will be more or less side branches upon them. It is best to cut most of these off—all the largest, at least, as by doing this we preserve the equilibrium between root and top, as more or less roots are destroyed in taking up, besides the cutting off the lower portion of the main root.

Trees grown from cuttings will have no tap-root, and consequently will not require the same pruning as seedlings. But they will usually have much larger and stronger side roots as well as branches. Both should be shortened, to make them more convenient for handling as well as planting. The general from which such trees will naturally take can be readily seen when young, and the pruning should be made in accordance with the purpose for which they are intended. The trees may now be planted in nursery rows, where they can be cultivated, or where they are wanted for a forest. They will be better if planted in a nursery and well cultivated for a few years, say until they are four to eight feet high, and then planted where it is intended they should remain. The root pruning and transplanting when young, as well as the after-cultivation, makes the plants throw out an abundance of fibrous roots, which enables us to transplant them in after-years with the greatest ease and success.

CHAPTER VII.

TRANSPLANTING LARGE TREES.

SOMETIMES it will be desirable to transplant large trees, and whether from the nursery or forest, the roots will be more or less broken. The ends that were cut off by the spade will be left very rough. Before being planted again, these broken roots should be removed, and the ends made as smooth as possible, for it is from these wounds that most of the new roots are formed. If the roots are left in a rough state, the water enters the pores and they soon commence to decay; and when this once begins, it will very often continue until the whole root is dead, and disease communicated to the tree that will sooner or later be the means of destroying it. I consider root pruning of so much importance that I never plant a tree of any kind, large or small, without first examining the roots, making every rough end and bruised spot smooth. Never plant a tree that has any dead or diseased roots; better have but a part of one good, sound root than a dozen that are unhealthy.

When roots are so long as to make it inconvenient to plant the tree and have the roots spread out at full length, they may be cut off, always making the cut from the under side upward and outward. Fig. 14, B, shows a root properly cut, and A, one improperly. When roots are cut off in transplanting, a corresponding quantity of the branches should be removed. If no roots have been destroyed, having been moved from the soil where they had become fixed, it requires some time for them to adapt themselves to their new position and draw sufficient sustenance from the soil to support a new growth.

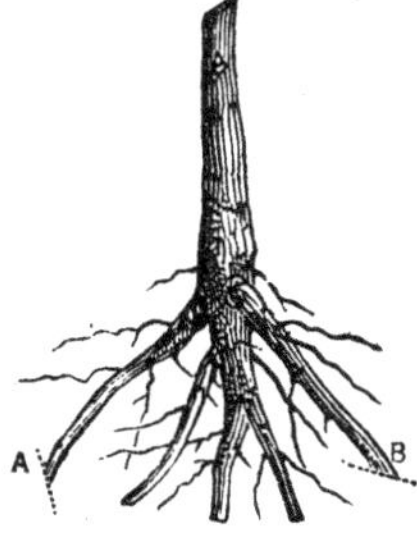

Fig. 14.

Because roots are *in* soil is no evidence that they can take up that which they need from it, for they require contact by growth before they can absorb plant-food to any considerable amount. It therefore becomes indispensable that we should remove a portion of the branches, that they may not call for more nutriment than the roots are capable of supplying. It may not be positively necessary to save the life of the tree or insure a rapid growth, still experience proves it to be beneficial, although some theorists have labored long and faithfully to convince the practical planter who freely amputates roots and branches that he does not understand his business.

The novice in these matters has only to ask himself the question, What is my object in performing this or that operation? in other words, keep *thinking* as he progresses with his work. If he wants his tree to grow low and spreading, he must see that it is necessary to give it room to do so, and if it does not take that form, cut off the leading shoot and compel it. If he wants the opposite, then trim off the lower branches, and not give the tree so much room to spread.

Every one who has ever seen a forest must have observed that the more crowded the trees the more slender in growth—the upper branches seeking the light, and the lower ones dying for the want of it.

Never cut away a branch unless you can satisfactorily to yourself answer the question *why*. In such matters I would much rather trust to the common sense of the novice (if he will use it) than to the professional gardener who walks in the path which has been made for him by others, and who is afraid to deviate for fear of losing his way.

It is not a general practice to prune evergreen trees at the time of transplanting, but with most kinds it can be done with safety and with benefit. Evergreen trees usually do not extend their roots so widely as the deciduous trees, consequently they are more readily taken up entire, therefore obviating to some extent the necessity of lessening the branches.

When planting a tree of large size, say from ten to twenty feet high, and one that has large lateral roots, we should endeavor to make the soil under it of such a consistency that it will settle evenly—not more in the center than upon the outsides, for in that case there would be a vacuum left under the center of the tree, which should be avoided. If the roots are not sufficiently strong to hold up the tree and the soil above, then they become bent and thrown out of their natural position, which in most trees is at a slight angle from the stem downward.

Very few persons will go to the expense of properly preparing soil for the reception of trees. Underdraining and thorough subsoiling should always be done if it is clay or heavy loam. Some will endeavor to make up for their

Fig. 15.

neglect by digging large, deep holes, filling them up with good soil, and on this plant their trees. This is a very good plan, and the larger they are made the better. But on clayey soils they often become mere reservoirs that receive all the surface-water for several yards about the tree, making a mud-hole instead of a dry place.

The shape in which holes are generally dug is only making a bad matter worse; that is, making them deeper in the center than upon the outside, so that when filled up to the proper height to receive the tree, there is a greater depth of loose soil under the center, where there is less use for it, than at the extremities of the roots. The proper shape in which to leave the subsoil in the bottom of the hole is in the form of a dome. When the hole is filled up to where you wish to set the tree, you have less loose soil under the center than at the extremities of the roots, which entirely obviates the difficulty mentioned above. As the water passes down through the soil and reaches this cone, it settles away from the tree instead of remaining under it. Fig. 15, A, shows the form of the bottom of the hole when ready for the tree. If a post auger is bored down in two or more places around the outside of the hole, B, B, it will be found very beneficial in carrying off the surplus water. Some may object to this form of leaving the bottom, as it will not leave as much room for the center or tap-root. But we are supposing that the trees have been carefully prepared when young, and the tap-root cut away at the proper time.

In planting trees of large size, it becomes necessary that we should use some means by which we can keep them firm in their places until fibrous roots obtain a better hold of the soil than they had when first planted. The oscillating of the stem displaces the roots, and though but little, it will often be sufficient to break the connection of the young rootlets with the soil, thereby cutting off the sources through which food must come. To prevent this, a great variety of means have been employed. The usual method is to plant a stake with the tree, reaching several feet up the stem, and make the two fast together with some bark, straw, or soft rope. Sometimes two stakes are employed. being driven a foot or more from the tree on opposite sides, and the tree made fast to these with rope or straw ties. Another method is to drive four stakes on opposite sides and several feet from the tree, and from these extend a strong wire to the upper portions of the stem. This, without doubt, is the surest means of keeping the tree in its place, and especially for those kinds which have few if any large roots. But it must be remembered that plants as well as animals need exercise, and no tree will remain healthy or grow as vigorously in a position where it can not have the exercises which Nature designed it should, though it is very probable that depriving the stem for one season of the slight movement which it naturally receives would not injure it to any conceivable amount. But these appliances are not very ornamental, and are sometimes very inconvenient, especially when you wish to cultivate the ground about the tree, which should be done the first year after planting, if no longer. I have practiced the following method of staking large trees that have strong lateral roots, and find it answers the purpose better than any other I have tried. Make some stakes, two or more feet in length, of good strong wood, leaving a branch four or five inches long on one side, and about the same distance from the end—fig. 16. If trees are not handy to make these from, some plank will answer as well, cutting a notch in the edge. When the tree is placed at the proper depth, drive these stakes down by the side of the largest roots so that the hook will clasp and hold the root firm. See fig. 15. Three or four of these will be sufficient for each tree, unless they are very large. Fill up the hole as usual, covering up the stakes; they will rot away in two or three years; if not, they will do no harm. By following this plan you have no wires or other unsightly machinery in view, leaving the stem and branches free, while the roots are kept as firm in their place as could be desired.

Fig. 16.

DEPTH TO PLANT TREES.

No tree taken from nursery or forest should be planted ny deeper than when in its original position. But as the newly moved soil will usually settle somewhat, both that which is under as well as that which is put over the roots, it is best to provide for this by placing the tree a little higher in the soil and covering the roots a little deeper so as to allow for this settling.

PLANTING TREES FOR SHELTER.

In selecting trees for shelter, much depends upon the

amount of land to be used for that purpose. If only a few feet in width can be spared, then those kinds must be selected which will afford the most protection for the space occupied. When only a narrow belt is to be planted, then evergreen trees are the most suitable. Soil and situation will also determine in a measure what particular varieties are best adapted for the purpose. Some kinds will grow almost equally well upon low, wet soil as in a high and dry situation, while others make but a poor growth if planted in any soil which differs much from the one in which they naturally grew. Hemlock will grow in a low, wet situation, provided there is a gravelly or stony subsoil; but they will seldom attain a large size, and they will always be more or less diseased. A moist, deep loam is the best suited to them—a cold, clayey soil the very worst. Arborvitæs, White Cedar, and Balsam Fir will do well on low land. The Arborvitæ will also do well on quite dry soil. The Balsam Fir and White Cedar do moderately well, but prefer a moist soil. Therefore, in planting a belt of trees, if the soil is variable, use trees of different kinds, unless one kind is preferred and the preparation of the ground to suit is not an objection. The Hemlock is certainly one of the most beautiful of evergreen trees. No foreign variety excels it in graceful foliage or richness of color. I would place this at the head of the list of evergreen trees for the purpose of shelter or as a single specimen tree. It grows well when planted in masses, and never looks stiff and formal when grown in large belts or hedges. It is of rapid growth, and transplants with ease when grown in a nursery from seed. There are various other kinds which will also make an excellent screen, but I can not name them all in this place.

To make a screen that will not occupy more than ten feet wide only, a single row should be planted. The trees should be at least three feet apart for a healthy growth, and if they remain in the nursery until they are four to six feet high, they should be planted four to six feet apart. If planted upon very dry soil, it is well to mulch the surface of the soil for three or four feet wide on each side the row; or, in place of this, keep the surface of the soil loose and free of weeds with a hoe for two or three years, or until the lower branches spread sufficiently to shade the ground. Always plant when the soil is moist, but not wet, and take up the trees with as much soil adhering to the roots as possible. Late spring, after the ground has become settled, is the best time to transplant evergreen trees at the North.

Some persons trim their evergreen trees, when planted in belts, so as to give them a hedge-like appearance. This is a matter of taste; but for my part I prefer an undulating, irregular appearance to that of a stiff, monotonous one, which is often seen displayed where we would least expect it. A hedge is one thing, and a belt of trees for protection is quite another. Two or three rows of trees are much better, when the land can be spared, than a single row; besides, it gives a more solid and noble appearance to the place which it surrounds.

When two or more rows are planted, the trees may be planted farther apart, and alternately, as shown in diagram, * * * * * *; or when three or more rows are used, following the same plan, thus giving an equal space to each tree. When we get beyond four or five rows, then some of the deciduous trees may be employed with the evergreens, but it is better not to intermingle them, but place them on one side, as this mode is much preferable to mixing together, as is sometimes done. If you form groups, then evergreen and deciduous trees may be planted together, as sufficient space can be given each for full development. It will often occur that only a large single group of trees is wanted to break the wind from some particular direction. In such cases grouping the different varieties of evergreen trees, interspersed with the deciduous, would certainly give a more pleasing effect than to have it made up of any particular kind; but the arranging of groups belongs to the landscape gardener, upon whose grounds I do not wish to trespass—at least not here. Deciduous trees are not so suitable for protection as evergreens, unless planted in large numbers. It will, however, often be economy to plant them in situations where they will afford shelter, and at the same time be growing for other purposes.

If a rapid growth is required, it is best to plant in rows, not only for convenience in cultivating them while young, but as they are thinned from time to time, the spaces between the trees can be left more uniform, allowing each to occupy a certain amount of room. Trees which have equal space on all sides will grow more uniformly than when crowded on one side and an abundance of room on another. How far apart trees should be planted at the beginning, must depend upon the purpose for which they are grown. If they are of a kind which will be valuable when young, then plant very thickly, and thin out as required; but if only wanted when they become large, then plant at a considerable distance, for if allowed plenty of room, they will of course grow more rapidly than when crowded. The value of some kinds of timber is increased by the rapidity of its growth, but with other kinds, that which grows most slowly is the best.

A Locust or Red Cedar that grows forty feet high in ten years is not so good as one that takes twenty years to reach that height. But a thrifty, rapid-growing Hickory is much tougher and better than one that grows very slowly.

MIXING VARIETIES.

Planting several kinds together is an old English custom, the utility of which is at least questionable. No two varieties will grow with equal vigor upon the same soil, consequently the more rapid growing are constantly encroaching upon the weaker. If a variety requires protection, then plant a kind which does not need it in such a position as to afford that protection, but do not intermingle them. Let each kind be entirely separate, and still the weak will be benefited by the close proximity to the stronger.

CHAPTER VIII.

PRUNING OF FOREST TREES.

THIS is another subject upon which there has been much discussion, and the more the subject is agitated the greater becomes the number of opinions and theories. While the trees remain in the nursery rows they require annual prunings in order that we may have them of the proper shape when required for permanent plantations. It is not desirable to prune them severely, but only to give the growth the proper direction. Sometimes there will be several leading shoots, and the tree will assume the shape of a shrub more than of a tree. In such cases, all the shoots, except the strongest, should be cut away close to the main stock. All suckers from near the base of the tree should be annually cut off. The trees should also be trimmed up —that is, the lower branches cut off smooth to the stem, epecially when the trees are wanted for timber. A straight stem is always desirable, and it can not be had with some varieties unless the knife is frequently used. If the trees are properly pruned when young, there will be no necessity of taking off large branches when they become old. Too many branches must not be taken off at one time, as leaves are indispensable to growth; but young trees may produce more leaves than is necessary for a healthy growth, and a reduction in number may increase rather than decrease strength, as it will enable those leaves that remain to enlarge and act with more vigor than if all had remained. Some varieties will require but little pruning, while others imperatively demand it at least once a year, or very little progress will be observed.

Pruning should not be practiced to such an extent that the tree will be eventually weakened or checked in growth. Neither should too many of the lower branches be taken off at one time, but expose the stem gradually to the sun. A tree when grown in the open field will usually produce branches sufficient to shade the whole of its stem. This appears to be not only natural but beneficial, for when the stem is fully exposed to the sun the bark becomes dry and hot, and the flow of sap is retarded in its circulation. It is only while young and the bark thin that any particular injury will be perceived. The stems of trees do not require the direct rays of the sun, but the leaves can not exist long without them.

When trees are grown in nurseries, the stems are partially shaded, consequently the lower branches are not required for shade, but only to assist growth until a sufficient number of others have been produced, so that their services can be dispensed with without injury to the tree.

Trees when standing alone should have at least two thirds of their height occupied with branches. But when grown in thickets, and for the purpose of producing timber, this rule may be reversed, and the branches occupy only one third, varying the rule according to the natural habit of the tree. If it is one of those which produce a conical head, like the Balsam, Tulip, and Larch, then allow one half the height for the branches. Any one who will observe the natural habit of a tree will soon learn how it should be pruned to make it serve the purpose for which it is wanted. It can be made crooked or straight, with many stems or one, for trees are not so intractable as is sometimes supposed.

I think there is little need of my warning the novice in forest tree culture of the injury which may result from pruning too much, because we see that there are too many cases of failure from not pruning enough, even among those who profess to thoroughly understand the laws of vegetable physiology.

We often see young trees that have become stunted in growth, and no amount of manure or cultivation will set them growing. Many a professional gardener will give physiological lectures upon their case, explaining the reason of their perversity, when, if he would take his knife and cut the tree down to the ground, or severely head it back, it would make a growth of several feet before he gets through with his lecture, or searching for reasons why the nitrogen and ammonia in the manure, or the superphosphate which had been applied, did not act on the vital functions of the tree.

PRUNING EVERGREENS.

Evergreen trees will submit to the knife as well as deciduous trees; but as they are not likely to be so generally grown for timber as the others, it will not be necessary to go into detail as to the best method of pruning them. As a general rule, they should not be pruned when young, unless it is for the purpose of giving them some particular shape. When several leaders are produced, the tree grows too broad in proportion to its height, then take out all but one; or if any side branches grow beyond and out of proportion to others, cut them back. They may be headed back or trimmed up to suit our purpose; but this pruning may be delayed until the tree has become well established and five to ten feet in height.

The planter has only to keep in view the object to be obtained: If the trees are wanted for long, straight timber, then long, erect stems will be required; but if for screens, than preserve as many lower branches as possible, to give density to the tree.

When trees are grown for ornament, and are given plenty of room, very little pruning is required, as they will usually take a natural form, which is always more beautiful to those who have acquired a correct taste than any distortion that may be given by the pruner.

Every tree-grower should study the natural habits of the tree, and then he can mold it to his liking and make it subservient to his wishes.

TIME TO PRUNE.

Pruning should never be performed at a time when the sap will flow from the wound, as this would not only weaken the tree, but the exuding sap covers the wound, and often causes the exposed wood to decay. Our object, therefore, should be to choose a time when the tree will not bleed (as it is termed), and the wound made will be covered with new wood the soonest. For this purpose there is no better time than in summer, after the leaves have become fully formed and the tree has commenced to make a new growth. The wound made will have sufficient time for healing over, or partially so, during summer, and few trees will bleed at this time, and none enough to injure them.

Pruning may also be done any time in summer, fall, or early winter, but should not be performed in the latter part of winter or just as the spring approaches, for at this season there is more or less danger of the trees bleeding. Some varieties may be pruned at any time without any apparent injury, and those kinds from which the sap flows but very little may be pruned in winter, any time before the cold weather has passed, as one cold night will so dry the wounds that no sap will exude. There are other kinds, like the Maple, which, if wounded in winter, will be most sure to bleed at the approach of warm weather. Midsummer is the best time to prune all resinous trees, as well as those that produce gum.

When trees are transplanted, they should be pruned at the time, as no tree will bleed after the roots have been separated from the soil. If we cut off a branch of the Birch or Maple in early spring, the sap will flow very rapidly from the wound; but if we dig up the tree, the sap will cease flowing in a few moments.

IMPLEMENTS USED IN PRUNING.

The common pruning-knife is the best implement for pruning small trees; but when large branches are to be removed, a fine tooth-saw may be used, always smoothing the wound with a sharp knife or chisel. An application of some material which will cover the wound and exclude water, is often beneficial where large wounds are made, but it is not necessary when only small branches are taken off. Various compositions are in use for this purpose, but common grafting-wax applied when warm, or gum-shellac dissolved in alcohol and applied with a brush, will exclude the air perfectly until there will be but little danger of decay.

CHAPTER IX.

TIME TO CUT TIMBER.

It is not to be supposed that the intelligent farmer who may at any time be in want of a stake for his sled or grapevine will wait until some particular season before he cuts it; neither will he consult some old-time almanac to learn whether the sign is right, or the moon is of the proper age—for such superstition belongs to the past, as the moon has not the influence on vegetation that our grandfathers believed in their time. There are, however, certain seasons in which it is more convenient to cut timber than in others.

Many persons assert that if a tree is cut in October or November, the wood will be much more durable than if cut in April or May. Under some circumstances this may be true; in others, it is not. In the spring the sap is in a fluid state, and the outer portions of the tree contain more water than in autumn, consequently if cut at this time, and no opportunity given it to get rid of this excess of moisture, it will decay more rapidly than if cut when comparatively dry. The bark is also soft at this time, allowing those insects which deposit their eggs that produce the various worms—larvæ—a better opportunity for doing so. Every farmer will have observed that his Hickory and some other kinds of wood will be infested with worms and become (as often termed) powder-ported. The old Hemlock stumps and logs are often found quite filled with large, whitish worms of two or more inches in length. The Locust, the Wild Thorn-Apple, Beech, and many other kinds of trees, are much infested with borers, and very few trees are entirely exempt.

Some kind of insects attack the trees while they are growing, while others do so only when they are decaying. All these borers or worms are but the larvæ of some kind of winged insect hatched from their eggs, deposited in or under the bark or soft wood at some period of its growth or decay. Some species of these worms feed entirely upon live wood, while others upon that which is dead or decaying. The habits and appearance of most of these insects are well known to entomologists, and fully described in the various works on that subject.

When trees are cut down in the fall, the sap which was in a fluid state in the spring has now become wood, and the outer surface is comparatively dry, so much so that few insects have the power of inserting their ovipositor (egg placer) into or through the bark, consequently a less number of eggs will be deposited than if the tree had been cut in the spring. But when we cut small timber for posts, stakes, etc., it is always best to take off the bark, for if left on it will absorb and retain moisture to an extent that will hasten the decay of the wood. If cut in spring, the bark comes off readily and leaves the wood clean; but at any other time it is removed with difficulty. Thus there appears to be an objection to both seasons, and no intermediate one is any better. When large trees are cut, such as are suitable for hewn timber, boards, rails, etc., if placed in a position where they will soon become dry and seasoned, there is probably no choice in the season.

From the observation which I have been able to make in cutting and using more or less timber, from my boyhood to the present time, I have come to the conclusion that trees cut in spring and immediately stripped of their bark, and then exposed fully to the sun and air so that the surface will soon dry, will last as long and be as durable in any position as when cut at any other time.

All stakes and posts which are to be set in the ground should be stripped of their bark, certainly that portion which is placed under ground. When we consider the fact, that it is only the outer portions of the tree—the sap-wood, leaves, buds, and inner layers of the bark—which are really alive and contain true sap, all other portions being dead, and only serve as a covering or like the heart-wood sustaining the tree in its position, we can readily see why it will make no material difference in the lasting qualities of timber whether it is cut in the new, full, or old moon, summer or winter, provided the green portion is soon dried so that insects can not find a lodgment for their eggs, nor decay be accelerated by the presence of moisture.

We may have other objects in view besides the value of the timber taken, such as a second crop produced by sprouts from the old stumps; if so, then there are certainly particular seasons which are better than others. If the trees are cut in late fall or winter, the roots and stumps will throw up sprouts much more abundant and vigorous than if the trees are cut in summer when in full growth.

In fact, the latter period is just the time to cut off trees and small under shrubs if we wish to kill the roots. The exact time of year to cut timber to kill the roots can not be given, as the seasons vary as well as climate in the different latitudes. The right time here would not be the right time forty miles north or south. Many rules have been given, such as the three longest days, the old or the new moon in certain months; but these rules would not give the same results in any two States in the Union, nor hardly apply to any two species of tree or shrub, consequently they are useless. When trees or shrubs have *nearly* completed their new growth in summer, but not entirely, they will suffer more by being cut down than at any other time.

CHAPTER X.

DECIDUOUS TREES.

THE following list of trees is arranged alphabetically according to their generic botanical name.* I have followed Dr. Asa Gray in the names of most of our native trees, believing him to be the best authority extant, at least so far as regards the native trees of our Northern forests. But no full botanical description will be attempted, as this would necessitate the use of many words which are not generally understood, my object being only to call the attention of the reader to the most valuable native forest trees, also noticing a few of the best foreign species which are well suited to cultivation in the Northern States, the seeds of which can be readily obtained.

ACER. (*Maple.*)

A genus containing many species, most of which are trees of large size; only a few are shrubs. The Maples have palmated-lobed leaves, with the edges variously serrated (notched). Fig. 17 shows a leaf of the

* The word *generic* is from the Latin *genus*, and is applied to particular groups. For instance, Acer is the generic for the whole group of Maples. The specific name is applied to the different individuals of the group, and follows the generic name. Sugar Maple is called Acer Saccharinum, Acer being the generic, and Saccharinum being the specific or name of the species.

Red Maple somewhat less than natural size. Flower small, not very conspicuous; seeds in pairs, remaining together until ripe; each seed is furnished with a long winglike appendage. Seeds of this form are called keys, or by

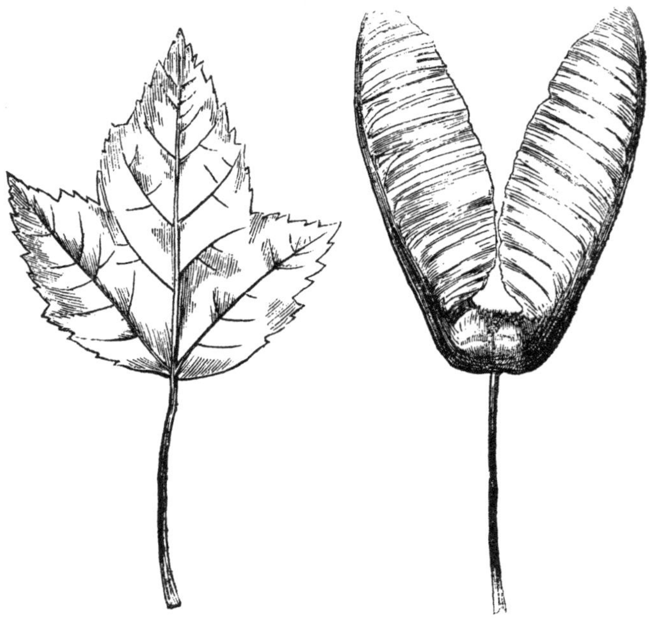

Fig. 17. Fig. 18.

botanists, samaras. In fig. 18 a pair of the Oregon Maple seeds are shown; they are somewhat larger than any of the species native of the Atlantic States.

ACER SACCHARINUM (*Sugar Maple, Rock Maple, Hard Maple*).—Leaves three to five lobed, deep green above and paler beneath; flowers greenish yellow, appearing with the leaves; wing of seeds ouite broad; ripe in autumn;

should be sown soon after being gathered, or placed in a cool place until spring. A well-known tree, possessing many valuable qualities, one of which is its sweet sap, from which large quantities of sugar are annually made. The wood is hard and firm, and much used in cabinet-work. Sometimes trees are found in which the grain of the wood has a wavy undulating appearance; it is then called Curly Maple. The wood is also one of the most valuable for fuel. A beautiful as well as valuable rapid-growing tree; often grows to the height of eighty feet; prefers a calcareous soil — that is, one in which lime abounds. Abundant in most of the Northern States, and in some of the mountainous regions of the South.

ACER NIGRUM (*Black Maple*).—This is only a variety of the last, and very similar to it in growth and general appearance, but does not come into leaf quite as early in spring as the preceding; seeds ripen at the same time, and should receive same treatment.

ACER PENNSYLVANICUM (*Striped Maple*).—Leaves three-lobed, quite pointed; flowers greenish yellow, appearing with the leaves; seeds ripen in autumn; a small tree, of no value for its timber, but quite ornamental; very common both North and South.

ACER DASYCARPUM (*White or Silver Maple*).—Leaves deeply five-lobed; deep green above and silver-white underneath; flowers reddish yellow, sometimes only pale yellow, appearing before the leaves; seeds ripen early in the season, generally about the time leaves are fully expanded, and must be sown soon after they are ripe, as they will keep but a short time. It is the most rapid growing of all the

Maples; will often grow twenty feet high in three or four years from seed; succeeds well in a great variety of soils, but prefers a rich, moist one. Its wood is fine-grained, and used for a variety of purposes; it is not so hard or valuable as the Sugar Maple, but the tree is of more rapid growth. The sap is sweet, but not sufficiently so to pay for gathering and boiling for sugar.

Some of the finest specimens of Curl and Birds'-eye Maple are obtained from this species. It is found more abundant at the West and South than at the East. Many thousands of this tree are annually planted in the parks and streets of New York and other Eastern cities. If the seeds are sown as soon as ripe, they will make a growth of one to two feet the first season. This tree deserves particular attention by those who are desirous of obtaining wood for fuel; although it is not quite as valuable for that purpose as some others, still it is good, and the rapidity of its growth more than compensates the deficiency in quality. When at maturity it is often sixty to seventy feet high.

Acer rubrum (*Red Maple*). — Leaves three to five lobed—the center one the longest; whitish underneath, but not so white as the Silver Maple; flowers usually deep scarlet or crimson, but sometimes pale yellow, appearing very early in spring before the leaves; seeds ripen early, about the same time as the Silver Maple, but are not quite as large. The small branches are also deep red in winter. Its wood is rather soft, and decays rapidly if exposed to the weather; sometimes used for cabinet-work, as occasionally fine specimens of Curl Maple are found among the larger trees. Very common in swamps throughout the country. Grows sixty to seventy feet high, with stem one to three feet in diameter. Fig. 19 represents a seedling Red Maple as it appears when but a few inches high, having produced but two pairs of leaves, the lower pair being those that were contained in the seed, and termed cotyledons.

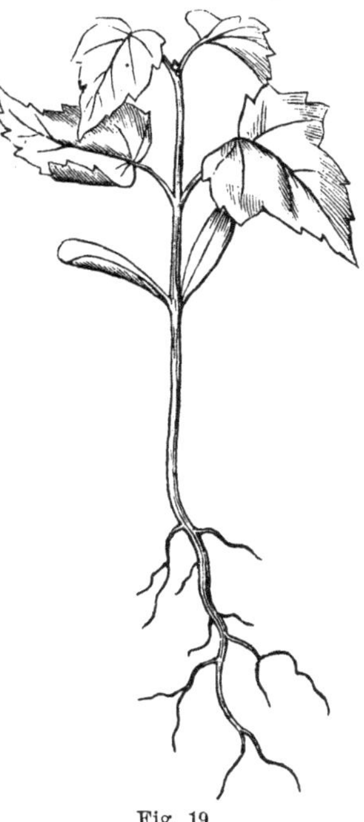
Fig. 19.

ACER SPICATUM (*Mountain Maple*).—This is only a tall shrub; very common at the North, but of no value for its wood.

ACER NEGUNDO (*Ash-Leaved Maple, Negundo Maple*).—This is sometimes called Negundo aceroides. It is a small tree with light yellowish green branches, used only as an ornamental tree; seeds ripen middle to last of summer; common West and South.

FOREIGN SPECIES.

ACER PLATANOIDES (*Norway Maple*).—Leaves similar in appearance to the Sugar Maple, but larger and of more substance; seeds ripen in the fall, and are considerably larger than our native species, except perhaps the Oregon

Maple. The Norway Maple is of slow growth while young, but grows quite rapidly after it is five or six years old. It is a very handsome tree, and well worthy of cultivation. Its wood is hard and fine-grained.

ACER PSEUDO-PLATANUS (*Sycamore Maple*).—A rather coarse-growing tree with large dark-green leaves. It is not a handsome tree, but is a rapid grower; its wood is hard and moderately fine-grained, and is valuable. Seeds are produced in long pendulous racemes; ripe in autumn, and require same treatment as others ripening at that time. Seeds of this and the preceding species can be procured from trees growing in this country. There are many other species of Maples, but those mentioned are the most common, and probably the most valuable for timber trees.

Maples, with but few exceptions, are readily worked one upon the other by budding. The Norway Maple grows more rapidly when budded upon the Sugar Maple. The Silver and Red Maple will also grow from cuttings, if planted early in spring in moist soil; the two or three year-old wood roots more freely than the one-year-old.

ÆSCULUS. (*Horse Chestnut.*)

There are none of this genus worthy of much attention, except for ornamental purposes. The trees are mostly of *small size*, and the wood of little value. Æsculus Hippocastanum, the common Horse Chestnut, is a native of Asia, but has been extensively planted in this country. Its beautiful flowers and the handsome foliage makes it generally admired. It grows to quite a large tree; leaves digitate, divided into seven leaflets.

ÆSCULUS GLABRA (*Ohio Buckeye*).—Leaflets five, as shown in fig. 20; flowers pale yellow; seeds large, nut-like, inclosed in a thick husk-like envelope, slightly prickly

Fig. 20.

when young; inside shell dark colored, shining. Seeds, ripe in autumn, should be but slightly covered with earth, or protected with leaves or other mulch; common in Ohio, Pennsylvania, and Kentucky; a slender-growing tree, forty to sixty feet high.

ÆSCULUS PURPURESCENS (*Purple Buckeye*).—A small-growing tree with dull purple flowers; common in the Southern States.

ÆSCULUS PAVIA (*Red Buckeye*). — Leaflets five to seven, smooth deep green; a small tree; much admired for its deep red flowers; Virginia and southward, although perfectly hardy in this latitude.

ÆSCULUS FLAVA (*Yellow Buckeye*).—Leaflets five to seven; flowers yellow; fruit large, smooth, ripe in autumn. This is the largest native species, sometimes growing to the height of seventy feet; Ohio, Indiana, and the South.

The seeds of the Horse Chestnut are all of large size,

from one to two inches in diameter, containing a large amount of farinaceous matter, which is very soon affected if placed in a dry situation or in a warm wet one. In a cool, moist situation they will remain sound for several months. Most of them ripen early in autumn, and should be immediately spread in a cool, shady place until wanted for planting. I have succeeded best by scattering the seeds in wide drills, and then filling the interstices between them with loose, friable soil, then covering them two or three inches deep with leaves. The most of these should be raked off in the spring; and so soon as the seeds have made an inch or two of growth (which they will do quite early), draw a little soil about them. The young seedlings have large, fleshy tap-roots producing few lateral ones the first season; and they should always be transplanted when young, and the tap-root shortened. Never allow them to remain in the seed-bed longer than two years. The Horse Chestnuts are readily worked one upon the other by budding; but as they generally make their entire growth early in the season, this operation must be done much earlier than with many other trees.

BETULA. (*Birch.*)

There are several native species of Birch, some of which grow to a large size. It is more common at the North than at the South. The wood is fine-grained, but not tough. Seeds produced in catkins, and are quite small, ripen in summer, and should be mixed with sand and kept until spring. Trees can also be propagated by cuttings, and succeed best in a moist soil. Leaves entire, usually quite thin; trees with a large amount of small spray, more or less graceful in habit.

Betula alba (*White Birch*).—Leaves triangular, taper-pointed; a small, slender tree with white bark; wood soft;

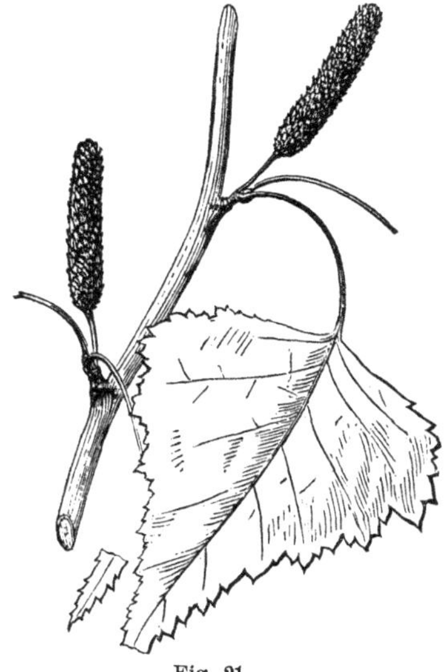

Fig. 21.

decays rapidly; of little value; common throughout the North in poor soils. The catkins of the B. alba as they appear the first season are shown in fig. 21. These remain till the second year, when the blossom and seed are produced.

Betula papyracea (*Paper Birch, Canoe Birch*).—Leaves heart-shaped, somewhat wedge-shaped, pointed; a large tree with fine-grained wood; bark very tough; formerly used by the Indians for making their canoes; common in the more Northern States and Canada.

Betula nigra (*Red Birch, Black Birch*).—Leaves broadly ovate, slightly pointed at both ends; downy underneath while young; a large tree with reddish-brown bark; wood fine-grained, compact, and heavy; succeeds best in deep alluvial soils; New England to Florida.

Betula excelsa (*Yellow Birch*).—Leaves ovate, or oblong ovate, pointed, irregularly and doubly serrate; tree forty to sixty feet high, with yellowish-white bark; young twigs slightly aromatic; wood of little value; Maine, Northern Michigan, and westward.

Betula lenta (*Sweet Black Birch*).—Leaves oblong, ovate, finely serrate; medium to large size; tree with dark-colored bark; wood fine-grained, dark reddish color; bark on young branches aromatic; mountains of Georgia, north and eastward.

Castanea. (*Chestnut.*)

This well-known nut-bearing tree is worthy of the attention of every land-owner in the country. It does not succeed equally well upon all kinds of soil; still, it is found growing over such a wide range of country, that there are probably very few counties in our Northern, Middle, or Western States in which soil suited to its growth can not be found. In the extreme northern portions of Wisconsin, Michigan, and Minnesota it would probably fail as it does in some portions of the Eastern States. It appears to prefer a dry, sandy, or gravelly soil to an alluvial, clayey, or very moist one. It will grow very rapidly, even upon a very poor sandy soil. Rocky hillsides, where soil can be found sufficient to start it, may be covered with this valuable tree. Its nuts always command a large price; and the past season (1865), $9 00 per bushel were paid in New York city for hundreds of bushels. I believe the time is not far distant when this tree will be planted in large numbers upon land that is now considered almost worthless; and one crop of the nuts from a twenty-year-old tree will more than pay for the original cost of the land and of planting them. It requires quite a large tree to produce a bushel of nuts, but not a very old one. If we allow forty feet square to each tree, we can then plant twenty-seven to the acre; and allowing only a half bushel to the tree, and five dollars per bushel, we have a return far above that of thousands and tens of thousands of acres of cultivated land in the Eastern or Western States. That it will require several years for the trees to grow to a bearing size is quite true; but we are now supposing that they are to occupy land that now brings no return; if so, there is no loss in waiting, except the interest on the small amount invested in the trees and labor of planting. If we plant it upon land that is cultivatable for other crops, we should plant thickly at first, and then thin out as they become large enough for use. So soon as the young trees are four to six inches in diameter, they are wanted for grape trellises, stakes, rails, posts, fuel, and a thousand other purposes for which wood is indispensable. There are other kinds of timber which may be more durable than chestnut, but I know of none that is more rapidly and easily grown. When the tree becomes large, it is even more valuable then when young.

We have only to look into the work-shop of the cabinetmaker to see it converted into many useful articles of furniture. We can scarcely go into a railroad car, steamboat, or hotel without seeing chestnut timber employed in some article of furniture or portion of the structure. Where toughness is required, or a very fine polish, chestnut will not answer, for it is naturally brittle and very coarse-grained; still, it will receive a polish sufficient for ordinary work, and it is now much used for finishing rooms; and when in connection with black walnut it produces a fine effect.

When a Chestnut tree is cut down, sprouts will almost invariably spring up from the old stump and grow with surprising rapidity (especially if the tree is cut in winter), so that a forest once planted is for all time. If these sprouts are thinned out when small, so as not to crowd, they will grow from four to six inches in diameter and thirty feet high in ten years. The Chestnut is also a very ornamental tree, with either a broad, oval, or cone-shaped head. It is variable in form: sometimes it will branch low and form a round, globular-shaped head, such as shown in fig. 22, which is

Fig. 22.

an exact representation of a tree growing near Paterson, N. J. The leaves are from five to seven inches long and two to three broad, tapering to both ends and coarsely serrated. Fig. 23 shows a chestnut leaf about one half the natural size. Fertile flowers, very small in clusters, inclosed in a scaly involucre which surrounds the nuts. The sterile flowers are in long, naked catkins in clusters. The nut proper is inclosed in a thin horn-like covering. Fig. 24 shows one of the common chestnuts, natural size.

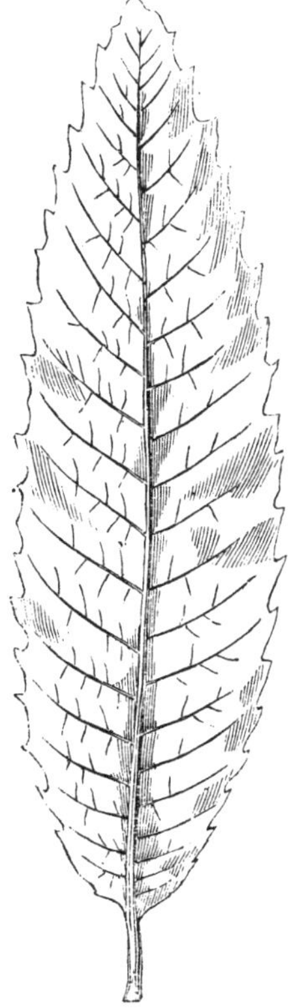

Fig. 23.

Fig. 24.

CASTANEA VESCA.—The Spanish Chestnut is a variety of this species. It is not quite as hardy as our American variety, but will grow as far north as Central New York. The nuts are much larger than our native kind, but not as sweet.

The Chestnut is readily grafted or budded. The annular budding is often employed, but I have never found any difficulty in grafting them with the ordinary clef graft.

Castanea pumila (*Chinquapin*).—This is a small-growing species of the Chestnut found chiefly at the South, but occasionally as far north as Pennsylvania. It seldom grows more than twenty or thirty feet in height; nut quite small, sweet, solitary, and not in threes, as in the other species. When worked on the stronger-growing kind, it grows more rapidly than on its own roots.

Our common American Chestnut, C. vesca, was at one time supposed to be a distinct species, but Mr. Gray now classes the European and American, with the exception of C. pumila, as one species. There are a number of foreign varieties to which particular names have been applied, such as Golden of Syria, Marie de Lyon, Chataigne Exalade, Downton, Prolific, and some twenty others; but the real distinction between these varieties are more in name than in the fruit. Scarcely any two trees of our native Chestnut produces nuts alike, and any number of varieties could be selected if it were desirable to multiply names. There will probably be new and valuable varieties produced that will deserve distinct names. All of the European varieties produce larger nuts than our native ones, but none of them are as good. The nuts of the foreign as well as native kinds can be procured of almost any seedsman. Plant in fall, and treat same as the Horse Chestnut.

Carya. (*Hickory.*)

The Hickory is another well-known tree possessing many valuable qualities. Its wood has no equal for fuel, and it is employed in almost every branch of mechanics where tough timber is required. A volume might be filled with merely the names of the articles which are wholly or in part made of hickory. There are several species, some of which are to be found in almost every portion of the United States, and in almost all kinds of soils, high or low, wet and dry. Sand-stone regions have their hickories as well as the limestone, but seldom of the same species, all of which are more or less valuable. Hickory hoop-poles are always in demand, and command a large price. Plantations for this purpose alone would be very valuable. For ornamental purposes, there are few trees that excel the Hickory in variety and beauty of foliage.

Fig. 25.

The Hickories are chiefly rather coarse-growing trees, with very little small spray, the branches terminating with a large bud. Fig. 25 shows a terminal shoot of C. tomentosa as it appears in spring, before the leaves expand. The leaflets are situated on a long petiole with three terminal ones, the others in opposite pairs, consequently there is an odd number of leaflets, often variable in the same species. Fig. 26 shows a hickory leaf with seven leaflets. The nuts are produced usually in clusters, inclosed in a thick leathery husk, which divides when ripe and allows the nut proper to fall out.

CARYA OLIVÆFORMIS (*Pecan-nut*).—Leaflets eleven to fifteen, oblong lanceolate; nut long, oval, as seen in fig. 27, nearly smooth; shell very thin; kernel sweet and good, but inclosed in a thin, brownish-colored, brittle substance that is intensely bitter; tree a slender grower, but

Fig. 26.

handsome; wood not as valuable as some of the more Northern species; native of Southern Illinois and southward. This species deserves to be extensively cultivated for its excellent nuts, which always command an almost exorbitant price in the Eastern cities. The past season the retail price in New York was eighty cents per quart.

Carya alba (*Shell-bark or Shay-bark Hickory*)—Leaflets five, slightly downy on under side, obovate lanceolate, serratures small; nut medium size, as shown in fig. 28—

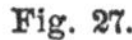
Fig. 27.

Fig. 28.

sometimes large; surface uneven, white; shell thin; kernel large; an excellent, well-known tree; grows to a large size; bark rough, shell-like; wood tough, very valuable; common in the Eastern States, and in some localities at the Northwest.

Carya sulcata (*Thick Shell-bark Hickory*).—Leaflets seven to nine, in form like the preceding; nut prominently ribbed, slightly flattened, of a yellowish color, and quite a thick shell; kernel sweet and good; common in Kentucky and Illinois; tree of large growth; wood tough and valuable.

Carya tomentosa (*Mocker-nut, White-heart Hickory*).—Leaflets seven to nine, oblong, sometimes nearly lanceolate, slightly serrate, rough underneath; nut globular, nearly smooth, sometimes slightly ribbed; shell very thick, of a brownish color; kernel small, sweet; tree of large size, with a rough furrowed bark on old trees, but quite smooth when young. This is probably the most abundant of all the Hickories, being very common from New England to the Mississippi and westward. Its wood is tough and light-colored, there appearing to be very little of what is usually termed heart-wood, even in the largest trees. The nuts of this species are variable: on some trees not more than three fourths of an inch in diameter, while on others they are two inches. The tree is well suited for growing upon high and dry soils, as it is generally found more abundant in such situations than in deep, rich soils.

CARYA MICROCARPA (*Small-fruited Hickory*).—Leaflets five to seven, oblong lanceolate, smooth; nut nearly round, small, inclosed in a very thin husk; shell also quite thin; kernel sweet and large in proportion to the size of the nut. Tree grows to a large size, and resembles the preceding species. Found occasionally in New Jersey, but more common in Pennsylvania and southward.

CARYA GLABRA (*Pig-nut*).—Leaflets five to seven, ovate lanceolate, smooth; nut somewhat pear-shaped, with a thin husk, which generally adheres to the nut after it has fallen from the tree; shell thick; kernel variable — sometimes quite sweet, in others bitter. A large tree with a smooth bark; wood tough, light-colored; common almost everywhere; abundant on the dry, sandy hills of New Jersey, and westward.

CARYA AMARA (*Bitter-nut, Swamp Hickory*).—Leaflets seven to thirteen, oblong lanceolate, serrate, smooth; fruit nearly round, but variable; shell thin; husk, with quite prominent ridges running nearly the whole length, thin; kernel intensely bitter; tree rather graceful; branches small; terminal buds small; covered in winter with a yellow pubescence. A terminal bud and small portion of a branch are shown in fig. 29. Common in low, moist soils; wood not as valuable as that of the other species.

Fig. 29.

The Hickories, as a class, are trees of comparatively slow growth while young. As found in forests, they do not bear transplanting very well, owing to their habit of producing a long tap-root with but few lateral ones; this difficulty is in a great measure obviated when they are grown in the nursery and properly root-pruned. They should always be transplanted from the seed-bed when one year old; and if it is intended to transplant them when they become large, it is best to move them every three or four years, carefully root-pruning them each time. This frequent transplanting is beneficial to all trees that are to be removed when they have become large; but none more imperatively demand it than the Hickory.

Cladrastis tinctoria. (*Yellow Wood. Virgilia lutea* of Michaux.)

Leaflets seven to eleven, oval, light-green, shining; flowers in long racemes, white, about an inch in diameter, pea-shaped—the racemes produced on the ends of the branches; bark smooth on young trees, becoming slightly furrowed on old ones; wood yellow, hence its common name. A beautiful and graceful ornamental tree of medium size, blooming when quite small, of slow growth for the first two or three years, after which it grows quite rapidly. Its seeds retain their vitality for a long time, germinate readily if sown in the fall, covering them about an inch deep. It prefers a rather dry soil, but one that is rich. It is a native of Kentucky, but not plentiful except in a few localities; and should be more generally known than it is at present.

FAGUS. (*Beech.*)

The Beech is a common tree in most of the Northern States. It grows to a large size, often from sixty to one hundred feet high and from two to four feet in diameter. The wood is well known, being used for a variety of purposes where a fine hard surface is required. Mechanics' tools, such as planes, saw-handles, etc., are almost exclusively made of beech. The wood is not tough, but extremely hard. It makes excellent fuel, and is also much used in some sections for building timber. The largest and best trees grow on deep, loamy soils, but it is common on dry, sandy, and stony ones, on which it seldom grows to any considerable size. The roots spread very widely, and keep near the surface, as every one who has cleared off beech lands well knows. The Beech is not a slow grower; still, it will require many years for the trees to become of an available size for fuel or timber, although the young trees may be used for hoop-poles. It is sometimes employed for hedges and screens, for which purpose it is most excellent, although it should not be planted where cattle can get to it, as they are very fond of its leaves.

The Beech has many excellent qualities, and although it is not one of most profitable kinds to grow for timber, still any one who contemplates planting forest trees on a

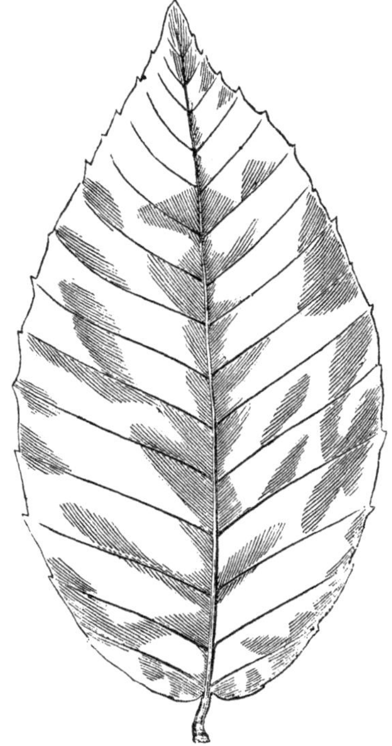

Fig. 30.

large scale should not overlook it. There is but one clearly defined native species described by Dr. Gray, although all botanists prior to him have supposed there were several.

FAGUS FERUGINEA (*Red Beech, White Beech, etc.*—

Leaves entire, oblong ovate—see fig. 30—coarsely serrate or toothed, deep green, shining as they become fully developed; seed triangular, produced in pairs inclosed in a rough, hard husk; kernel sweet and delicious, an excellent nut; tree variable in size; bark smooth, light-colored;

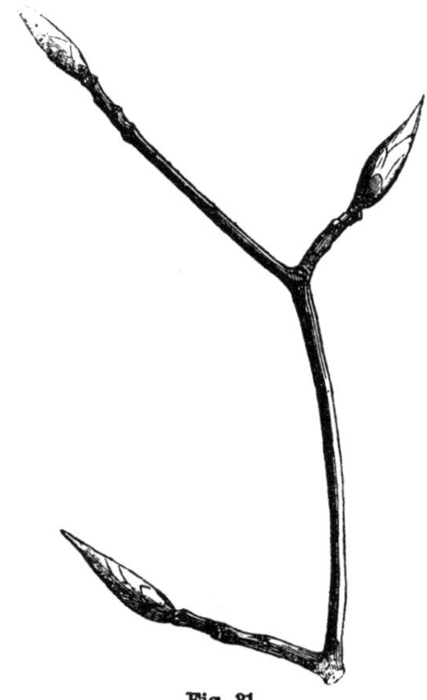

Fig. 31.

naturally of graceful habit, producing an abundance of light spray with taper terminal buds. Fig. 31 shows a small branch (natural size) from a large tree. A fine ornamental tree, deserves a place in the smallest collection. There are several varieties of the Beech which are quite distinct, among which are the Copper, the Purple, Weeping, Cut-leaved, etc.; these are to be found in the larger nurseries. They are propagated either by layering, or grafting or budding on the common variety. In grafting, it is better to use a portion of the two-year-old wood for the cion than to have it all of one-year-old. The nuts of the common Beech ripen in the fall, and should be treated the same as the Chestnut.

FRAXINUS. (*Ash.*)

There are several native species of the Ash, which, like the Hickories, are all worthy of cultivation. The wood is extensively used for all the different agricultural implements. Our reapers and mowers, plows, harrows, hoe and rake handles are, in great part, made of Ash. European farmers prize American-manufactured agricultural implements more than they do home-made of the same patterns, simply because we use better timber than they possess, and that timber is chiefly White Ash.

Fig. 32.

The Ash has what is termed a pinnate leaf, that is, divided into several small leaflets on a petiole. There is a great variety of pinnate leaves; the Locust is a well-known example of this form. Fig. 32 shows a leaf-stalk of the Locust with seventeen leaflets; in some kinds the number of leaflets is even, as we have shown, in others odd. In the leaves of the Ash there is always an odd number of leaflets, because there is a terminal one, and the others are in pairs, situated on opposite sides of the petiole or leaf-stalk. The leaflets shown in fig. 32 are all of the same size and shape; but in other forms of pinnated leaves the leaflets are variable, both in size and form.

Fraxinus Americana (*White Ash*).—Leaflets seven to nine, ovate or oblong pointed; young branches smooth; seeds produced in long, slender panicles, winged, or what is called key fruits; bark on old trees rough, deeply furrowed; tree of large size; wood very white, except the heart-wood in old trees; seeds ripen in autumn; should be sown soon after being gathered. It requires a moist, deep soil, in which it will grow very rapidly. It is a noble tree, and one of the most valuable; is also very ornamental, forming a large round head when grown as a single specimen. This species deserves the special attention of those who are growing trees for their timber; common in most of the Eastern States, but rather scarce at the West.

Fraxinus pubescens (*Red Ash*).—Leaflets seven to nine, oblong lanceolate, somewhat pubescent on the under side; not as large a tree as the preceding, and the timber inferior; native of the same localities.

Fraxinus verdis (*Green Ash*).—Leaflets five to nine, oblong lanceolate; upper ones serrate, deep green; tree of medium size; wood valuable; common in low grounds near streams throughout the Northern States.

Fraxinus sambucifolia (*Black Ash, Water Ash.*)—Leaflets seven to eleven, oblong lanceolate-pointed; seeds winged all around; tree a tall and slender grower, coarse-grained; and as it readily separates into thin layers it is much used for making baskets; common in low grounds in the Northern States; very plentiful in Central New York. Valuable for growing in low, wet soils.

FRAXINUS QUADRANGULATA (*Blue Ash*).—Leaflets seven to nine, with very short stalks, oblong ovate; young branches nearly square, hence the specific name; fruit an inch and a half long and three eighths of an inch wide; a large tree, producing very valuable timber; grows in dry uplands; common in Ohio and to the Southwest.

FRAXINUS PLATYCARPA (*Carolina Water Ash*).—Leaflets five to seven, ovate, slightly pointed at both ends; seeds with broad wings, smaller than the preceding; a medium-sized tree, growing in wet soils at the South.

All the different species of Ash grow readily from seeds and produce an abundance of fibrous roots the first season; consequently they are easily transplanted, even when they become of considerable size. There are several foreign species and varieties, many of which are cultivated as ornamental trees. These are readily worked on the more common ones. They may be budded or grafted, always using the free-growing sorts for stocks. The native species which deserve the most attention as timber trees are —F. alba and F. quadrangulata for high and dry situations; and the F. sambucifolia for low, wet soils.

GLEDITSCHIA. (*Honey Locust.*)

The Honey Locust has been much extolled as a hedge-plant, and quite extensively planted in some sections for that purpose. It is doubtful if it will ever become popular for this purpose as it is naturally a large tree, consequently requiring severe pruning to keep it in check.

There are many other plants better suited for hedges, and which do not produce such enormous thorns. If ever there was a tree that ought to be proscribed and exterminated, I believe this to be one. The thorns on old trees are often six to ten inches long, and so hard and sharp, that the man or beast that approaches them is in danger of being mortally wounded. Every little clipping from a hedge must be carefully picked up, or there is danger of some animal stepping on it and having its feet pierced by these natural bayonets.

The tree is quite ornamental, having beautiful deep-green pinnate leaves, which give it a very graceful appearance. The seeds are produced in long pea-shaped pods, and are ripe in autumn, and if sown at that time will grow quite readily. They will also retain their vitality for many years if placed in a dry place; but their tough, horn-like covering will become so hard in time as to be almost impervious to moisture, consequently old seeds require soaking in warm water before sowing. A good way is to pour boiling water on them, and let it remain where it will keep warm, but not hot, until the seeds swell. There are but two native species.

Gleditschia tricanthos (*Three-thorned Acacia*).—Leaflets lanceolate oblong, slightly serrate, deep green, smooth; pods a foot or more in length, usually twisted, with a sweet pulp between the seeds; tree of medium size, with a spreading open head; common in Pennsylvania and westward. There are cultivated varieties of this species without thorns.

Gleditschia monosperma (*Water Locust*).—Leaflets ovate; pods small, containing one seed; thorns simple;

tree of small growth; native of Southern States, found chiefly in swamps.

Gymnocladus Canadensis. (*Kentucky Coffee.*)

Leaflets seven to thirteen, ovate, borne on a leaf-stalk two to three feet in length; seeds about one half inch in diameter, produced in a pod of from five to ten inches long; ripe in autumn; may be sown so soon as ripe, or be kept until spring. I have succeeded best by keeping them in a cool cellar until spring, then planting, covering about an inch deep. It is a tall-growing tree, with large branches. Its appearance in winter is rather coarse, but when in full leaf it is stately and highly ornamental. It grows rapidly, and the wood is said to be valuable. It is but little known at the East as a timber tree, although the young trees are found in all of the principal nurseries. It is a native of Ohio and of the Southwest.

Juglans cinerea. (*Butternut.*)

Leaflets fifteen to nineteen, oblong lanceolate, rounded at the base, variable, not always directly opposite, as shown in fig. 32, page 95; petioles and small branches downy, with clammy hairs; fruit oblong, inclosed in a clammy brittle covering; nut deeply furrowed, with sharp point. Fig. 33 shows a nut of natural size, with the outside covering partially removed; kernel sweet, rich, and very oily. The Butternut seldom becomes a very large tree, although occasionally one will be found sixty to seventy feet high and two to three feet in diameter. Its bark is smooth until the tree becomes very old, then it is slightly furrowed. The wood is coarse-grained, of a light-brown color, and is much used in cabinet-work. Its nuts ripen

Fig. 33.

in autumn, and should be planted at that time. It is common in all the Northern States, and thrives best in moist, rich soils.

It would scarcely be worth the trouble to plant the Butternut for its timber, but every farm should have a few to produce nuts. Many of us can look back to the time in our boyhood when the cracking of butternuts and hickory nuts was the main feature in our evening enjoyments. Farmers, remember that a few Butternut trees may cause your sons and daughters to send a thought or a blessing back to the old homestead when far away and surrounded by the cares and anxieties which we all experience in our journey thorough life.

JUGLANS NIGRA. (*Black Walnut.*)

Leaflets eleven to twenty-one, ovate lanceolate, slightly heart-shaped at the base; fruit nearly round, rough, not clammy; nut furrowed, nearly black. Fig. 34 shows its natural size, with outside covering removed; kernel sweet,

Fig. 34.

with a strong flavor, much admired by some—to others it is quite disagreeable. It is a much more rapid-growing and larger tree than the Butternut. The bark on the young as well as old trees is dark-colored, and on large branches and stems very rough and deeply furrowed. Its wood is dark purplish brown, becoming almost black with age, and fine-grained, and may be highly polished; is much used for cabinet-work and for finishing houses. It is the darkest and richest colored of any of our native woods, and always in great demand. It does not require a very large tree to make a sufficient amount of lumber to bring a hundred dollars in New York. It is not very common in the Eastern States, but plentiful at the West. I have seen many a farm in Southern Illinois which was mainly fenced with black-walnut rails. It is probably not more than twenty years since these rails were cut, and there is little doubt that if the trees from which they were made had been allowed to remain until this time, one hundred of them would have been worth more than the same number ot acres of the cultivated land on which they formerly stood. This is but one instance among the many thousands where, to use an old adage, the goose that laid the golden egg has been killed.

The Black Walnut grows rapidly in good rich, soils. It should have plenty of room, as it has a wide-spreading and rather open head, with coarse, stout branches. It comes into bearing, like the Butternut, when quite young, producing nuts in abundance. Plant the nuts in autumn, and transplant when one year old.

The *Juglans regia*, or English Walnut—sometimes called Madeira nut, etc.—is a species of this genus. The tree very much resembles the Butternut, and one unacquainted with it would think it identical. The nuts, however, as they appear on the tree, are more like those of the Black Walnut. It is not quite so hardy as our native species; still, young trees seem to thrive as far north as Central New York; but I am not aware that any trees so far north have borne fruit. About New York city there are large trees that have borne for several years. The nut is well known in our markets, as they are annually imported in large quantities. Large plantations should be made of this tree in the Middle States, where it will thrive, and the nuts will pay well for growing. It is certainly poor policy to be constantly importing an article which we can produce with profit ourselves. We possess all the facilities—a suitable climate, abundance of land, and men, women, and children in our large cities who should be set to work at growing the young trees upon a large scale, instead of remaining as they now do, crowded in unwholesome tenement-houses, and doing nothing that benefits themselves or the country.

LARIX AMERICANA. (*Larch, Tamarack, Hackmatack.*)

The Larch is classed by botanists among the Coniferæ or cone-bearing trees, which are chiefly evergreen; but as this sheds its leaves in autumn, I have placed it here among the deciduous trees. The leaves are very small and thread-like, resembling some of the Pines. Fig. 35 shows two

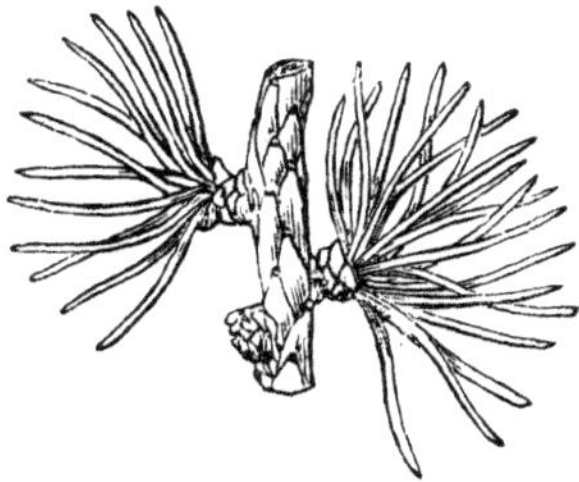

Fig. 35.

clusters of the leaves, natural size; seeds are borne in small ovoid cones; ripe in autumn. They should be treated the same as evergreen tree seeds—*i. e.*, sown in a half shady situation or in frames; tree a tall, slender grower; wood valuable, where light straight timber is required. It is also valuable for fuel, but burns rapidly. The trees should always be cut in winter or early spring and the bark taken off; unless this is done, it will decay very rapidly. Grows naturally in low grounds, in nearly all of the Northern States as well as in the Canadas.

The European Larch is a much more valuable tree, and should be planted in preference to the native species, as it thrives on dry soil and grows to a larger size, and the timber is much better. A volume might be filled with accounts of the many plantations which have been made of the English or Scotch Larch. Thousands and tens of thousands of acres have been and are still being planted in Scotland and other portions of Great Britain with this tree. These plantations have proved to be valuable investments, and in many cases—in fact, we might say in most of them—land that was of no value for ordinary farming has been used for this purpose.

Thousands of acres are now lying waste near our seaboard cities on which Larch would grow rapidly, and every tree is, and ever will be, wanted in every seaport. The Larch makes excellent spiles for docks, or for the foundations of buildings which are built in low, wet grounds. That it will last for ages when covered with water or driven in wet ground we have abundant proof. Larch spiles have been taken up in Europe where it is positively known that they were driven more than a thousand years ago, and yet they were sound and uninjured. Who will be the first to make a plantation of Scotch Larch on the barrens of Long Island or New Jersey? The seeds can be obtained of any of our seedsmen, and in almost any quantity, if the order for them is given a few months in advance of the time they are wanted.

I have noticed the Larch at length, and more particularly for the purpose of calling the attention of those who owr large tracts of the sandy soils of our Eastern States than for Western men, as there is more demand for it here than at the West; besides, we have such an abundance of land on which very few other varieties would grow rapidly enough to be as profitable as this. It should also be remembered that a plantation of Larch would improve the land instead of impoverishing it, as the annual crop of leaves deposits more nutriment than the tree takes up, a fact well known in countries where this tree is extensively cultivated.

LIRIODENDRON TULIPIFERA. (*Tulip-tree Whitewood.*)

Leaves smooth, on slender petioles, partially three-lobed, the middle one appearing as though cut off; flowers about two inches broad, bell-shaped, greenish yellow, marked with orange; seeds winged, in a large cone-shape cluster, which falls apart in autumn. Fig. 36 shows a single seed as it appears when separated from the mass. It blooms in May and June, and the seeds ripen in late summer or early autumn, and should be sown as soon as ripe in good, moderately dry soil. They may remain in the seed-bed two years, if desirable, but should receive a slight protection the first winter; tree of large size, sometimes one hundred and thirty feet high, with a very straight stem; wood light color, greenish-white, soft and light, not hard enough to receive a polish. It is much used in cabinet-work, and for making panels for carriages, and for any inside work where toughness or a hard surface is not required. There is perhaps no native wood that will shrink more in seasoning than whitewood, for it not only shrinks side-

Fig. 36.

ways, but endways as well; but when once thoroughly seasoned, it remains fixed, and does not warp or twist like many of the hard and tough kinds of wood. There is also much difference in character of the wood coming from different sections of the country, and mechanics who are conversant with the various kinds and localities will readily tell whether specimens came from the West or East. The latter is of a light greenish color, grain not so smooth and soft, and sometimes rather tough. To produce good timber, the soil should be deep and rich, and on such the trees will grow very rapidly. The wood is little used, except for the purposes mentioned above, consequently it is only large trees that will be of much value. It is one of the most beautiful ornamental trees we possess, growing in a conical form, and producing an abundance of its beautiful tulip-shaped flowers in spring. The roots are soft and sponge-like, and it requires great care in removing to insure success. Frequent transplanting in the nursery is the best method for preparing the trees for future removal.

LIQUIDAMBER STYRACIFLUA. (*Sweet Gum*—Bilsted.)

Leaves with five to seven lobes, somewhat star-shaped, lobes slightly serrate, deep shining green in summer, becoming a dark brown or crimson in autumn; young branches light gray, with prominent cork-like ridges; bark on old trees furrowed; seed-vessel round, nut-like, very rough, pendulous; seeds small-winged, mostly abortive, there being few perfect seeds, generally not more than three or four in each catkin or head; a large and beautiful tree, more abundant near the Atlantic coast than westward. It grows very straight, tapering gradually from the base upward. The wood is fine-grained, and when seasoned is split with difficulty; it has some valuable qualities, but not enough to be worthy of general cultivation; when small, it is easily transplanted, but as it becomes large it is quite difficult to make it live, even when moved with much care.

MAGNOLIA.

The Magnolias are all more or less valued for their beautiful foliage and flowers. Few if any of them offer much inducement to one who wishes to grow trees for timber only, and the whole of this genus more properly belongs to the ornamental than to the useful.

MAGNOLIA ACUMINATA (*Cucumber Tree*).—Leaves oval, pointed, six to ten inches long, downy beneath; flowers three to four inches in diameter, dull green tinged with yellow; fruit two to three inches long, cone-shaped, seeds imbedded in the outer surface. This is the largest of the Magnolias, growing seventy feet high; wood soft and fine-grained, resembling the Whitewood. It is used in some sections for making wooden bowls, trays, etc.; quite plentiful in the southern counties of Western New York, Ohio, and Pennsylvania.

MAGNOLIA GLAUCA (*Swamp Magnolia, Sweet Bay, etc*). —Leaves oval, shining above and white beneath; flowers white, two to three inches in diameter, very fragrant; fruit oval, one inch and a half long; a large shrub, very ornamental; common from New York to Florida, chiefly near the coast.

MAGNOLIA MACROPHYLLA (*Great-leaved Magnolia*).—

Leaves in cluster at the ends of the branches, oblong obovate, soft, whitish downy beneath, two to three feet long; flowers white, large, nearly a foot broad; fruit ovate, two to three inches in diameter; young branches large and covered with a white pubescence; tree of medium size, very irregular in growth; wood brittle, the branches easily broken by the wind; a noble-looking tree; native of Kentucky and southward, but hardy as far north as New York.

MAGNOLIA UMBRELLA (*Magnolia tripetela, Umbrella-tree*).—Leaves one to two feet long, ovate-oblong, downy beneath when young; flowers white, six to eight inches in diameter; fruit oblong, four to six inches long, rose color; young branches smooth, with very long terminal bud; tree thirty to forty feet high, spreading open head; a very handsome ornamental tree; found in same localities as M. acuminata.

MAGNOLIA FRASERI (*Ear-leaved Umbrella-tree*).—Leaves oblong ovate, eight to twelve inches long, somewhat heart-shaped at the base, smooth on both sides; flowers white, six inches broad; fruit oblong, smaller than in M. umbrella; the branches are also more slender; tree thirty to forty feet high; Tennessee and southward, but not very plentiful anywhere.

MAGNOLIA CORDATA (*Yellow Cucumber-tree*).—Leaves oval, slightly heart-shaped, downy beneath; flowers yellow, five inches broad; a wide-spreading tree with comparatively slender branches; common in Georgia and South Carolina; quite hardy in the latitude of New York.

MAGNOLIA GRANDIFLORA (*Great Laurel Magnolia.*—

Leaves oblong obovate, smooth, glossy above and dull white beneath, evergreen; flowers white, very fragrant; fruit three to four inches long; native of the South; not hardy north of Virginia, although occasionally a tree will survive for a few years as far north as New York.

There are several foreign species and varieties of Magnolias that are worthy of being cultivated in every garden. These, like the M. conspicua, M. Soulangiana, M. purpurea, etc., bloom before their leaves appear, which gives the tree a most magnificent appearance. These foreign species do not, as a class, grow as rapidly as the native ones, but they bloom when quite small. To give them increased vigor they should be budded on the Magnolia acuminata.

All the Magnolias may be propagated by layers, although plants grown in this manner are not equal to those grown from seeds or by budding. The different species are generally propagated from seeds; these are gathered so soon as they can be seen in the opening fruit or cones, which should then be spread out where they will dry sufficiently to allow the seeds to be shaken or picked out by hand. Then mix the seeds with sand, and put away in a cool cellar until spring, or sow immediately in a light sandy or loamy soil. The seeds will soon lose their vitality if allowed to become dry or remain in the fruit where they will become heated. Mice are very fond of Magnolia seed, and considerable care is often necessary to prevent them from getting a taste. The seedlings may be allowed to remain in the seed-bed for two years before being transplanted, as they grow rather slowly when young; besides, it is best to protect them the first winter, if no longer, and it is more convenient to do this while in the seed-bed than after being planted in the nursery.

NYSSA. (*Tupelo.*)

The Nyssas are trees of peculiar growth, the branches growing almost at right angles from the main stem, the upper ones often reaching as far outward as the lower, giving the tree a flattened appearance, as though it had met some obstruction which had prevented it from growing any higher. The grain of the wood runs in all directions, forming an intricate indivisible mass. This peculiarity of structure is its only value, as it is naturally soft and spongy. There are but two native species, although some botanists have divided the genus into several.

NYSSA MULTIFLORA (*Tupelo*, *Pepperidge*, *Sour-gum*).—Leaves oval, slightly pointed, pubescent when young, deep green, becoming dark brown or bright crimson in autumn; flowers in clusters, small, inconspicuous; fruit oval, bluish black, about one half inch long, ripe in autumn, should be sown soon after being gathered; tree medium to large; wood yellowish white, much used for wagon hubs, rollers, etc.; common in low, wet soils in all the Middle and Southern States; a slow grower, and hardly worthy of cultivation, except as an ornamental tree.

NYSSA UNIFLORA (*Large Tupelo*).—Leaves oblong, sometimes slightly heart-shaped at the base, downy when young; fertile flowers, solitary; fruit nearly an inch in length; a large tree with soft, spongy wood; common at the South, in low, wet soils.

PRUNUS. (*Plum and Cherry.*)

This genus contains many species, among which are the Wild Plums, both of the Northern and Southern States, besides a number of species of the Wild Cherry. Among them all there is but one species that grows to a sufficient size to be of any considerable value as a forest tree.

PRUNUS SEROTINA.—Leaves oblong, taper pointed, serrate, shining above; flowers in long racemes, white; fruit purplish black, sweet, slightly bitter; tree of large size; wood fine-grained, much used by cabinetmakers; common almost everywhere at the North; seeds ripen in summer and should be sown immediately, or in autumn at the farthest, as they are easily destroyed by drying; tree grows rapidly, but requires many years to become of sufficient size to be of much value except for fuel, and for this purpose there are many other trees that are far better. The Wild Cherry is infested by the tent-worm more than any other tree, and its cultivation should be discouraged at the East, unless stringent laws are passed compelling every landowner to exterminate the worms which may now be seen on every Wild Cherry tree in forest and fields as well as on the apple-trees.

PLATANUS. (*Buttonwood.*)

A well-known tree of the largest size. In some parts of the West, hollow trees of this kind were found by the early settlers of sufficient dimensions to shelter a whole family and make quite a comfortable habitation for themselves and stock. Very large specimens are still to be seen along our Western rivers, most of them being hollow.

there being only a few inches of the outer portions of the tree remaining, the inside having decayed.

Platanus occidentalis (*Buttonwood, Sycamore*).—Leaves angularly sinuate-lobed or toothed; seeds produced in a brittly, coriaceous nutlet, containing but one seed, which is ripe in autumn; the bark on old and young branches green, but separating in patches, leaving large white spots; tree of large size; wood fibrous, running in various directions and so interlaced that it can not be divided; wood not considered of much value, though sometimes sawed into planks and timber; may be readily propagated by cuttings, of either one or two year old wood; common throughout the Northern States.

Populus. (*Poplar.*)

There are a large number of species of the Poplar, none of which possess any particular merit as timber trees, unless it be that of rapid growth. Some of the species are used for ornamental trees, and have been since the days of the ancient Romans, when one of the species was so extensively planted in the streets and suburbs of Rome that it was called the People's tree, hence the name Populi or Populus. All the species and varieties are readily grown from cuttings, either of one-year-old wood or that which is three or four years old. Young branches or suckers of eight or ten feet long may be set in rows where they are wanted, and if the soil is kept moist, they will take root, and in this way quite a forest or hedge may be produced in one or two years; they prefer a moist soil, but will grow in a very dry one.

POPULUS TREMULOIDES (*American Aspen, Shaking Poplar, etc.*).—Leaves nearly heart-shaped, with long, slender stem; the peculiar form of leaf and stem allows them to vibrate with the slightest breeze; tree thirty to forty feet high; common in low grounds in most of the Northern States.

POPULUS GRANDIDENTATA (*Large-toothed Aspen*).—Leaves roundish ovate, with large tooth-like notches in the edges, woolly pubescent when young, becoming smooth in summer; tree medium to large; wood soft and very light when seasoned; Northern States and Canadas.

POPULUS HETEROPHYLLA (*Various-leaved Poplar*).—Leaves very similar to the last, but more variable in shape; tree of rather larger growth, often sixty to seventy feet high; common at the South; rare in the more Northern States.

POPULUS MONILIFERA (*Cottonwood*).—Leaves broadly heart-shaped; young branches angled; a large tree with soft, light-colored wood, of very rapid growth; its large foliage makes it quite a fine ornamental tree; very common in all the Western States, especially in Illinois.

POPULUS ANGULATA (*Angled Cottonwood*).—Leaves large, broadly heart-shaped, smooth, serrate with incurved teeth; young branches acutely angled, almost winged; a large tree; common at the West and Southwest.

POPULUS BALSAMIFERA (*Balsam Poplar, Tacmahac*).—Leaves ovate, gradually tapering to a point; young branches round, smooth; buds large, covered with a fragrant resinous matter in the spring, hence its name; often used for medicinal purposes; found only in the more

Northern States and Canadas. There is a variety of this species, P. condicans, or Balm of Gilead, which is quite scarce in its wild state, but common as an ornamental tree. There are several foreign species cultivated in this country, such as the well-known Lombardy Poplar (P. dilatata), and the Abele or White Poplar (P. alba), often called Silver Maple, as the leaves resemble the Maple in shape, and are covered with a white silky pubescence. It produces an immense number of suckers, consequently it becomes very troublesome, especially when planted on lawns. It grows very rapidly, and is quite ornamental; but there are many other kinds equally as beautiful which do not possess that very perplexing habit of producing suckers.

Quercus. (*Oak.*)

This is another genus containing a large number of species and varieties, among which are some of our most valuable timber trees. It would be impossible for me to fully describe them without employing the peculiar language and phrases used by botanists, which I fear would be understood only by very few readers. I shall therefore only notice a few of the most valuable species. The nuts or acorns of most of our Northern species ripen in the autumn of the first year; but the evergreen oaks of the South, as well as some of our Northern species, do not come to maturity until the end of the second year.

The forms of the leaves are variable; some are simple, resembling the Chestnut—these are called Chestnut Oaks, while others have deeply lobed leaves; the indentation or scollop is termed a *sinus*, hence the name, sinuate-lobed.

These lobes also have different forms, being round, pointed, toothed, etc. The White Oak (Q. alba) has oblong, obtuse-lobed leaves, as shown in fig. 37, but the form of

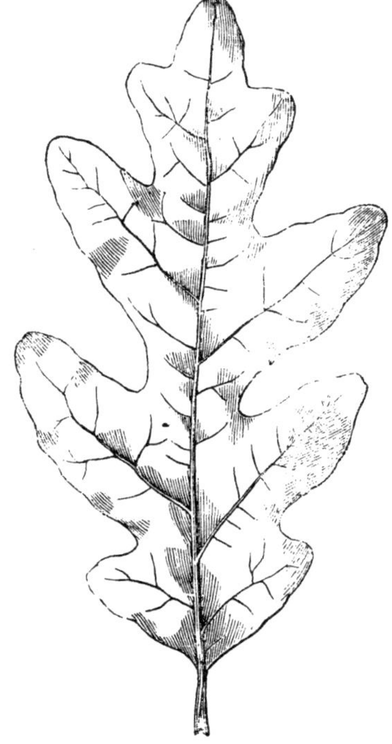

Fig. 37.

the whole leaf is obovate oblong. Another prominent characteristic, and one employed by botanists in determining the different species, is the acorns, some being small, with a sharp point, and set in a shallow cup like fig.

38; others are larger, and about half the nut inclosed in a cup, as in fig. 39; while in one species of Dwarf Oak the nut is almost entirely enveloped, as shown in fig. 40.

Fig. 38. Fig. 39. Fig. 40.

Taking these and the intermediate forms, and with the assistance of the leaves, we are able to determine which are distinct species without examining the other characteristics very minutely.

QUERCUS ALBA (*White Oak*).—Leaves obovate oblong, bright green when mature, cut into three to nine moderately deep, roundish lobes, as shown in fig. 37 page 115; acorn oblong, set in a rough saucer-shaped cup, see fig. 39. Acorns are variable in flavor—sometimes sweet and quite good, in others bitter, or almost tasteless. The bark on young trees is rough, but not furrowed, becoming somewhat scaly on old trees; color grayish white; wood light color, very tough and valuable. The White Oak is rather a slow grower, but the wood is so valuable that it deserves to be extensively planted. Take away the White Oak and White Ash, and American farm implements would lose two of the most valuable materials which enter into their composition. It requires a deep, rich, and dry soil to produce timber of the best quality.

QUERCUS OBTUSILOBA (*Post Oak*).—Leaves five to six inches long, with five to seven roundish lobes, and wide, open sinuses, pubescent beneath, petiole short; acorn about one half inch long, oval, about one third of its length being inclosed in the cup; tree of medium size; wood very tough, valuable; common in poor soils, both North and South.

QUERCUS MACROCARPA (*Mossy Cup Oak*).—Leaves eight to twelve inches long, with seven to nine deeply sinuated lobes, the lobes rounded, sometimes toothed, pale pubescent beneath; acorn large, scales on the cup thick, the upper ones long, fringe-like. On the rich lands of the West the acorns grow to a very large size, and are much sought after in some sections for making household ornaments; tree of medium size; more plentiful at the West than elsewhere.

QUERCUS PRINUS (*Swamp Chestnut Oak*).—Leaves oblong, or obovate oblong, coarsely toothed, smooth, shining above, pale pubescent beneath; acorn about one inch long, cup rather shallow, rough, with tubercled scales; common in low grounds at the South. A handsome tree, but wood not equal to some of our Northern species.

A variety of this species called Q. monticola, or Rock Chestnut Oak, is found in New York, Ohio, and Pennsylvania, as well as in the Southern States. It is a handsome tree, and the timber is valuable. Q. discolor, or Swamp White Oak, is also a variety of this species. Its leaves are more deeply sinuate-toothed than Q. Prinus.

QUERCUS CASTANEA (*Yellow Chestnut Oak*).—Leaves oblong acuminate, sharply toothed, very smooth above, slightly downy beneath, resembling the Chestnut more than the other species; acorn one half to three quarters of an inch long, three eighths to half an inch broad; cup with fine scales inclosing about one third of the nut; a medium-sized tree, quite handsome, and worthy of cultivation. New England to the Mississippi and southward.

Quercus prinoides (*Dwarf Chestnut Oak*).—This is only a small shrub, not worthy of cultivation.

Quercus Virens (*Live Oak*) and Quercus cinerea (*Upland Willow Oak*) are evergreen species, natives of the Southern States; not hardy at the North.

Quercus Phellos (*Willow Oak*).—Leaves two to four inches long, very narrow, tapering to both ends, resembling the leaves of some species of willow, smooth on both sides when fully grown; acorn small; cup shallow, merely inclosing the end of the hemispherical nut; tree forty to sixty feet high. Southern New Jersey and westward, also in Florida and Alabama. The acorns of this and the next species do not ripen until the fall of the second year.

Quercus imbricaria (*Shingle Oak*).—Leaves lanceolate oblong, acute at both ends, smooth above, slightly pubescent beneath; acorn nearly round, small; cup inclosing about one third of the nut; tree forty to fifty feet high; wood coarse-grained, much used by the early settlers at the West for shingles.

Quercus aquatica (*Water Oak*).—Leaves obovate oblong or wedge-shape, smooth on both sides, partially three lobed at the summit; acorn small, set in a shallow cup, tree of medium size, and found chiefly in low, wet grounds at the South.

Quercus nigra (*Black-Jack Oak*).—Leaves very large, broadly wedge-shape, mostly three-lobed at the summit, very dark green above, shining, dull, rusty pubescent beneath; acorn short, medium size; cup top-shape, very rough, inclosing one half of the nut; bark on the branches and stem deeply furrowed and of a very dark color; a beautiful tree when in full leaf; wood is coarse-grained, and not considered valuable except for fuel. It is common on the sandy soils of New Jersey, but is scarcely more than a large shrub there, while on the rich soils of Illinois it attains the height of forty to sixty feet.

QUERCUS TINCTORIA (*Quercitron Oak*).—Leaves obovate oblong, deeply sinuate-pinnatified, the lobes somewhat toothed, rusty downy when young, smooth at maturity; acorn spherical, three quarters of an inch long; cup shallow; kernel of nut extremely bitter; a large tree with thick bark—the inner layer is used by dyers; wood reddish, coarse-grained, much used for hewn timber. It is a native of most of the Northern States.

QUERCUS COCCINEA (*Scarlet Oak*).—Leaves with long petiole, oval with deep, broad sinuses, with six to eight entire lobes, bright green on both sides; acorn globular, about three quarters of an inch long; cup inclosing about one half its length; a large tree, with leaves becoming bright scarlet in autumn; grows in high, dry, but rich soils; common both North and South.

QUERCUS RUBRA (*Red Oak*)—Leaves oblong with shallow sinuses, slightly pubescent when young, becoming smooth; acorn large, ovoid, set in a very shallow cup; a large tree, with rather smooth bark until it is very old; wood very coarse-grained, not considered valuable; common in rocky woods from Canada to Florida.

Quercus palustris (*Pin Oak*, *Spanish Oak*).—Leaves oblong, smooth and shining on both sides, deeply lobed or pinnatified, with sharp acute teeth. A leaf of this species is shown in fig. 41. A very handsome medium-sized tree,

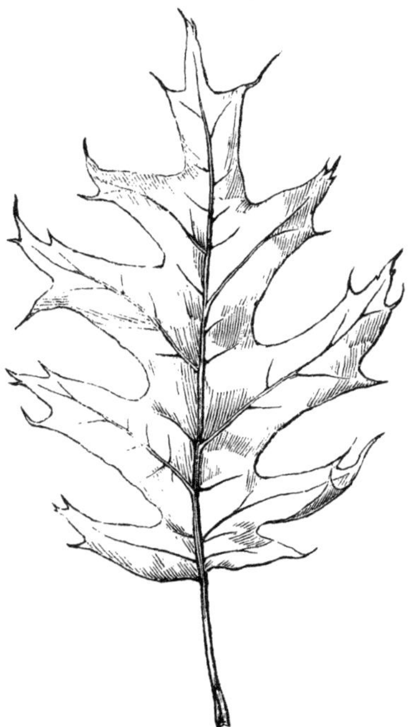

Fig. 41.

with smooth bark and rather slender branches which grow at almost right angles from the stem, sometimes drooping, giving the tree a unique and beautiful appearance. The wood is of good quality, often very tough. Another peculiarity of this tree is, that the stem tapers very rapidly from the base, more so than in any other species with which I am acquainted. It succeeds best in low, moist soils, and is common in New Jersey and westward.

The Oaks are all easily grown from seed; all that is required is to gather the acorns so soon as ripe and plant them in good soil, covering only a half inch deep. They should be transplanted when one year old, as they will then produce a large, fleshy tap-root; but unless transplanted when young, they will throw out but few lateral roots, continuing to penetrate the soil almost perpendicularly. I have seen tap-roots on comparatively young trees that were six to ten feet long. The most valuable species to be grown for timber are the Q. alba and Q. obtusiloba for high, dry soils, and the Q. Phellos, Q. imbricaria, and Q. palustris for low, wet soils.

ROBINIA. (*Locust.*)

The common Locust has probably been more extensively planted for its timber than any other tree in this country. Many acres were formerly planted on Long Island and New Jersey, and the remnants of these plantations are still to be seen in these localities. The usual practice was, to scatter the seeds in the original forests, leaving them to take root as best they could; when they had grown to a few feet in height, the native trees were cut out, leaving the Locust. In a few years these seedling Locusts became large enough to be cut and sold to the ship-builders or used for fence-posts. The Locust of this section of the country will remain sound in almost any position for an incredible length of time.

A few years since I took up an old fence which was built nearly or quite fifty years ago, and although the posts were not more than five inches in diameter, they appeared to be almost as sound as when first planted, not more than half an inch of the outer surface being decayed.

Some twenty years since, the Illinois farmers had a mania for planting locust for hedges as well as for timber, but for the former purpose it proved to be a failure, and for the latter but little better, as it was found that when grown in the deep, rich prairie soils its durability was much inferior to that grown on the sandy soils of Long Island and New Jersey.

The tree is of very rapid growth, and soon becomes large enough for use; but it has several faults as well as many good qualities. It produces seeds in great abundance, which become scattered, producing innumerable quantities of thorny shrubs, usually just where they are not wanted. It also produces a great number of suckers, and often at a great distance from the main stem. Another most serious objection to growing the Locust at the present time is that a species of borer attacks it in such numbers as to almost annihilate it in many sections of the country. If the ravages of the borer should cease, then the Locust would become one of the most profitable trees which could be selected, especially for the poor sandy soils of the Atlantic States. The seeds should be sown in the fall.

Robinia Pseudacacia (*Common Locust*).—Leaves odd, pinnate, with nine to seventeen oblong-ovate leaflets; flowers white, in long racemes, very fragrant; seeds produced in a long pea-shaped pod; young branches with short, stout thorns; bark on old trees rough, deeply furrowed; wood fine-grained, very hard, of a yellowish color; tree grows fifty to sixty feet high, and is commonly cultivated and indigenous to Virginia and westward.

Robinia viscosa (*Clammy Locust*).—Leaflets eleven to twenty-five, oblong; flowers white, tinged with red, in short crowded raceme; young branches clammy; tree of small size; common in cultivation, also on the banks of streams in South Carolina and Georgia.

Robinia hispidia (*Rose acacia, Moss Locust*). — A small, crooked-growing shrub with large pink or rose-colored flowers — a very handsome ornamental plant. When grafted on the common Locust, it blooms more profusely, and it forms a more beautiful shrub then when grown on its own roots.

Salix. (*Willow, Osier.*)

There are some twenty or more indigenous species of the Willow, but they are mainly small shrubs, and not worthy of being cultivated for their timber. There are, however, a few foreign species which have been so long in cultivation here, that they have become naturalized in many sections of the country; some of these grow to a large size, and are worthy of cultivation. All of the different species and varieties of Willow grow readily from cuttings, and they are usually propagated in this manner, except a few of new ornamental varieties; these are grafted or budded on other kinds.

Salix alba (*White Willow*).—Leaves lanceolate, pointed, covered with small silky hairs; young branches grayish white; tree a rapid grower, fifty to eighty feet high. The common Golden Willow is a variety of this species; native of Europe, but common in cultivation and along the banks of streams in all of the Eastern States. The White-Willow mania has been quite prevalent for the last few years, a few nurserymen having sent out numerous agents to extol it as a hedge-plant. That it will grow rapidly and form an impenetrable hedge in a few years is indisputable, but that a tree which naturally grows to sixty feet high can be kept within the bounds usually allotted to hedges is questionable at least. It is doubtless worthy of cultivation for its timber, but for hedges or screens there are many native shrubs and trees which are far better.

Salix Babylonia (*Weeping Willow*).—The very name of this tree sends our thoughts back to olden times, when nations destroyed nations and war was the chief employment of man. It has been a favorite tree with all civilized nations, and there is scarcely a poet from Virgil down to the present time who has not woven its praises into verse. It is certainly a beautiful tree, and when introduced sparingly among other trees, or beside a stream, pond, or fountain, it is not surpassed. When planted in large masses on grounds of limited extent, or in long, straight rows, as we often see it by the roadside, it produces anything but a pleasing effect. The Weeping Willow and

Lombardy Poplar are the two extremes in the great tree family—one is all tears; the other, a stoic of the tallest kind. The following are some of the most beautiful ornamental varieties—Rosemary-leaved, Ring-leaved, American Weeping or Fountain, Kilmarnock, and Golden Variegated.

Taxodium. (*Cypress.*)

The Cypress is one of the few deciduous coniferous trees that are indigenous to the United States. It grows to a very large size in the Southern States, particularly in the rich alluvial soils adjacent to the large rivers of that section. There is but one species east of the Rocky Mountains.

Taxodium distichum (*Cypress*).—Leaves linear, very small, numerous, two ranked on a very slender stalk; cones globular, about two inches long, with thick scales; seeds two-angled; bark pale-colored, smooth; wood light, but very durable; tree grows very rapidly, with a straight stem. Although this tree is a native of the Southern States, seldom being found in quantities north of Virignia, yet it is perfectly hardy as far north as New York. The valuable qualities of the Cypress have been in a great measure overlooked by those who require stakes in gardens, nurseries, or vineyards. Good cypress stakes can be grown much cheaper and at home than one could transport them ten or twenty miles, even if they cost nothing more; besides, the convenience of having a supply always at hand when wanted is not a small item. Red cedar stakes, eight to ten feet long, in the vicinity of New York, are worth from sixty to eighty dollars per thousand; and cypress stakes can be grown to that size in five or six years from seed, and they are almost as durable. Ten thousand cypress trees can be grown on an acre if planted in rows four feet apart and one foot apart in the row, and if they are worth but five cents each at the end of five years, it will give us a return of five hundred dollars per acre; and allowing fifty per cent. of the amount for cost of seed and cultivation, we then have a fair return for the use of the land. The Cypress is not very particular as to soil, but it will grow more rapidly in moist soil than in dry, but the wood is not so durable as when only a moderate growth is obtained. I have grown them successfully on high, dry, gravelly soils, where scarcely any other tree would thrive, and I am quite certain that any one can grow their own stakes much cheaper than they can usually buy them. The young trees should be cut in spring, and the bark taken off; then place them where they will become seasoned before they are used. Seeds can be obtained very cheaply at the South, and occasionally from seedsmen at the North. Sow in the open ground, either in spring or fall. The young seedling makes but few lateral roots the first season, consequently they should be taken up in the fall and carefully heeled in until spring, and then planted in the nursery rows.

TILIA. (*Linden.*)

Trees with large, handsome foliage and soft, light wood; much used when sawed into boards in sections of the country where it is abundant. All the species and varieties are very ornamental, and deserve especial attention for that purpose. Seeds ripen late in summer or early autumn; should be sown immediately after being gathered. The seedling produces many small fibrous roots, and is not difficult to transplant.

TILIA AMERICANA (*American Linden, Basswood*).—Leaves nearly heart-shape, large, thick, deep green on both sides; flowers yellowish; fruit a small, round, woody nut, with long peduncle; bark on young trees smooth, of a light green or gray color, becoming rough and deeply furrowed on old trees; wood white, soft, and very light when seasoned. A very large tree, common in all the Northern States and as far south as the mountains of Georgia. The inner bark of this species is much used by nurserymen for tying in buds, grafts, etc., and is commonly called Bass. The imported Bass mats are made from a species of this genus. To prepare the bark for use, it is stripped from the trees in spring, about the time the leaves begin to expand, when it comes off very readily; it is then put into water—a running stream is best—and allowed to remain there until it will separate into thin layers; two to four weeks will usually suffice for this purpose; it should then be taken out, stripped of the outside bark, and laid up in a dry place until wanted for use. Bass strings are excellent for tying up vines, raspberry plants, etc. The bark of all the different species may be prepared in the same manner.

Another valuable property of the Basswood is its very sweet, honey-bearing flowers. Those persons who keep the honey-bee for pleasure or profit should certainly plant the Basswood plentifully within reach of their bees, for there is no flower of its size which yields better honey or in greater abundance. In Western New York, the farmers who keep bees value their basswood honey equally with that of the white clover.

Tilia heterophylla (*White Basswood*).—Leaves very large, six to eight inches broad, smooth and bright green above, silvery white beneath; tree of more graceful habit than the first. There are several foreign species in cultivation that are well worthy of attention, such as the Tilia Europea, T. lutea, T. laciniata, etc. The small-growing varieties may be budded on those of stronger growth.

Ulmus. (*Elm.*)

There is probably no tree (the Oak excepted) which has been more extolled than the Elm, and full well does it deserve the praise. Noble, graceful, ornamental, and useful, then why should it not receive the homage of all nations who are so fortunate as to possess it? In Europe, great cities, towns, and noblemen's country seats have received their names from the Elm; and in the United States we have at least fifty villages and post-offices which have derived their name from this tree. But it is equally true that, with us at least, it receives more praise than patronage, for a hundred are cut down to one that is planted. This should not be, for it deserves to be extensively cultivated for ornament as well as for its valuable wood.

The seeds ripen in spring soon after the leaves expand. In this vicinity (New York) the Elm blooms in April, and the seeds are ripe by the first to middle of June, and they are usually scattered by the wind soon after they mature.

To secure them, they must be gathered so soon as they change to a brown color and the kernel becomes firm. If they are sown soon after being gathered, a greater portion of them will germinate in a few days and grow to a foot or more in height the first season. But a few of the seeds will sometimes remain in the ground without growing until the following spring, showing that they are not so fragile, and possess greater vitality than the seeds of the Silver and Red Maple, which ripen at the same time. The seeds are very small and light, and have thin membraneous wings that completely surround them, consequently they are very widely scattered by the wind, if allowed to fall from the tree.

ULMUS FULVA (*Slippery Elm*).—Leaves ovate oblong, serrate, thick, rough upper surface, soft, downy beneath; young branches pubescent; flowers greenish, appearing before the leaves; tree of medium size, with heart-wood red, rather soft and brittle; not considered so valuable as the next. The inside bark is used for medicinal purposes; common in low grounds both North and South.

ULMUS AMERICANA (*White Elm*, *Weeping Elm*).—Leaves obovate oblong, sharply serrate, thin, slightly pubescent underneath when young, becoming smooth; branches smooth, slender, often drooping; flowers purplish, in clusters on a slender-drooping peduncle.

It is the largest of the native Elms, often growing to the height of eighty feet, with stem of six to eight feet in diameter; a lofty and wide-spreading tree with a profusion of slender drooping spray. The wood is tough, and much valued by carriage-makers, for cabinet-work, etc.

The young trees of eight to twelve inches in diameter are extensively used for wagon and carriage hubs, and by many persons are thought to be unequaled for that purpose, as the wood is fine-grained, hard, and not liable to check or crack open, as with many other kinds. It is well worthy of cultivation, both for its wood and for ornament. The young seedlings have an abundance of small fibrous roots and are easily transplanted; common along streams from Canada East to Florida; also in the Northwestern States.

ULMUS RACEMOSA (*Corky White Elm*).—Leaves obovate oblong, serrate, green on both sides, not pubescent; young buds downy, with small hairs; flowers in a raceme; young branches sometimes with corky ridges; tree of large size, with very tough, fine-grained wood, valuable. New York, Ohio, and Michigan.

ULMUS ALATA (*Winged Elm, Wahoo*). — Leaves rather small, oblong lanceolate, sharply serrate, quite rough on upper surface, soft pubescent beneath; flowers in clusters on a slender stem; seeds oval, downy on the edges; rather a small tree, with tough, fine-grained wood. Virginia and southward.

The ULMUS CAMPESTRIS—English Elm—is also a valuable tree, and considerably cultivated for ornament, besides many varieties and species which are to be found in the larger nurseries.

The Elm delights in a deep, rich, and rather moist soil, and in such situations it will grow very rapidly, and the roots will extend to a great distance, completely taking possession of the soil. As there are few trees that can successfully maintain their ground when competing with the Elm, it is best to give it plenty of room, and it will soon make as much shade or timber as half a dozen crowded specimens would produce. It is also best to remove them from the nursery rows when quite small. If allowed to remain until they are ten feet high, the roots, which are very numerous, will form an intricate mass, which it is very difficult to extract from the soil without seriously injuring a large portion of them.

CHAPTER XI.

SMALL DECIDUOUS TREES.

THE following list comprises the most useful and ornamental varieties of native trees of small size, very few of which grow to more than thirty feet high. Most of them are desirable for ornament; besides, they will make excellent screens, forming an almost impenetrable barrier to winds when planted thickly, and they are generally better for protection than trees of larger growth. There is also less danger of their being blown down by hurricanes, as

> " ——— the storm,
> That makes the high elm couch and rends the oak,
> The humble lily spares. A thousand blows,
> That shake the lofty monarch of the forests,
> The lesser trees feel not."

ALNUS. (*Alder.*)

There are numerous species of the Alder, but most of our native ones are mere shrubs, and of but little value. Some of the larger-growing foreign species might be introduced and cultivated with profit, as they now are in many portions of Europe. The only native species found east of the Rocky Mountains that deserves any notice is the following—

ALNUS INCANA (*Speckled Alder*).—Leaves very broad, oval, sharply serrate, sometimes toothed, downy beneath; seeds produced in catkins—see fig. 42, which shows a cluster of its catkins: B, before they open; A, when in bloom. The catkins are formed early in spring, and remain naked through the summer and following winter, expanding the next spring; wood valuable for fuel; char-

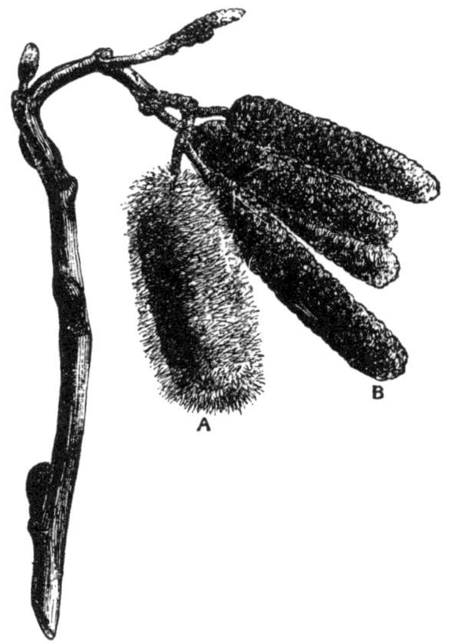

Fig. 42.

coal made from Alder is highly prized by manufacturers of gunpowder; grows in low, wet soils on the banks of streams; seeds ripen in early summer, and should be sown soon after being gathered. It also grows readily from cuttings, which should be planted in spring. This species is a native of both Europe and America.

Asimina triloba. (*Pawpaw, Custard Apple.*)

Leaves oblong ovate, acuminate, eight to ten inches

long, covered with a dull, rusty pubescence when young, at length smooth; flowers one to two inches broad, dark red or purple; fruit oblong, yellow and pulpy when ripe, edible; seeds large oval, flattened. Fig. 43 shows a seed of natural size. The tree grows from ten to twenty feet high, very ornamental; the fruit is much esteemed by many persons. The inside bark of this tree is much used at the West for strings for tying up vines, etc., as it is very tough. Its seeds ripen in autumn; may be planted at that time, or kept in a cool cellar until spring. They should be separated from the pulp soon after the fruit is gathered. Common in Ohio, Indiana, and southward.

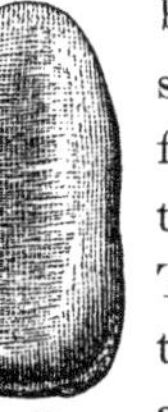
Fig. 43.

ASIMINA PARVIFLORA (*Small-flowered Pawpaw.* — A Southern species of low growth; both fruit and flowers much smaller than the first; fruit somewhat pear-shaped; probably not hardy at the North. The A. grandiflora and A. pygmea are also Southern species, found chiefly in Florida and Southern Georgia; not hardy in the Northern States.

ARALIA SPINOSA. (*Hercules Club.*)

Leaves very large, bipinnately compound; leaflets thick, ovate; flowers greenish, in a large loose panicle, succeeded by a small round berry which ripens late in summer; stem and branches covered with stout prickles; young shoots large, not branching, more curious than beautiful; may be grown from seeds or from cuttings of the roots; cultivated in many gardens at the North, and plentiful in Virginia and to the Southwest.

BERBERIS. (*Barberry.*)

The Barberry is a shrub of medium size, and I notice it here merely to call the farmer's attention to one of the best hedge-plants we possess. It is very hardy, and is naturalized in many portions of the New England States, but probably introduced from Europe. It forms a dense shrub of from four to eight feet high, with many slender upright branches covered with sharp stout prickles. It requires but little pruning to make an almost impenetrable hedge. The Barberry produces few or no suckers, except from the main stem. Its seeds ripen in fall, and should be sown in wide drills, and transplanted into hedge-rows when two years old, or at one year old, if desirable.

BERBERIS VULGARIS (*Common Barberry*).—Leaves obovate, bristly serrate; flowers in long drooping racemes; fruit oblong, scarlet, with an agreeable acid flavor, sometimes used for tarts; common in cultivation.

BERBERIS CANADENSIS (*American Barberry*).—This is a smaller-growing variety then the first, hardly strong enough for hedges. Virginia and Georgia.

CARPINUS AMERICANA. (*Hornbeam, Iron-wood, Blue Beech, Water Beech.*)

Leaves oblong ovate, pointed, serrate; fruit a small ovoid nut, ripe in autumn; a small tree with smooth bark and hard, very tough wood. Common in low grounds—well known.

CERCIS. (*Red Bud.*)

Small trees or shrubs blooming very early in spring, before the leaves expand. There are several foreign species and varieties in cultivation, all of which are much admired, and none more so than the Cercis Japonica and our native one.

Cercis Canadensis (*Red Bud, Judas Tree*).—Leaves heart-shaped, deep green, shining; flowers reddish purple, small, pea-shaped; seeds small, in pods, ripe early in summer, will retain their vitality for years, but grow more readily if sown soon after they are gathered; tree an irregular straggling grower. Common in the Western States; abundant in Southern Illinois.

Celtis occidentalis. (*Nettle Tree, Hackberry.*)

Leaves ovate, taper-pointed, sharply serrate; a small tree, of no particular value or beauty; fruit dark purple, sweet, ripe in autumn.

Catalpa bignonioides. (*Catalpa, Catawba Tree, Cigar Tree, etc.*)

Leaves large, heart-shaped, downy beneath; flowers bell-shaped, white, with purple spots in the throat, produced in long racemes, showy and handsome; seeds in long pods—which hang upon the tree all winter—and may be gathered and sown in the fall or spring; tree an upright, coarse, and rapid grower; wood brittle. Native of the Southwest, but common in culture at the North.

Chionanthus Virginica. (*White Fringe Tree.*)

Leaves oval, or obovate lanceolate; flowers in slender open panicles, very small but numerous, pure white; fruit about one half inch long, purple, ripe in autumn.

There is a variety of this with narrow leaves, which blooms more profusely, and the flowers smaller but intensely white; common in Virginia. When worked on the Ash, it makes a more beautiful tree, and grows more rapidly than on its own roots.

CORNUS. (*Dogwood.*)

A genus that contains many native species as well as several foreign ones that are cultivated for ornament. The only native species that grows large enough to be classed among trees is

CORNUS FLORIDA (*Flowering Dogwood*). — Leaves ovate, pointed; flowers greenish, small, inconspicuous, but inclosed in a large pure white involucre, which is generally supposed to be the flowers by those who are not acquainted with their structure; fruit oval, bright red, ripe in summer. Blooming as this tree does, in early spring, before the leaves expand, gives it a very showy appearance, rivaling the well-known Chinese Magnolia (M. conspicua); trees of twenty to thirty feet high, with fine-grained, very hard wood; common in the Northern States in high, dry soils; plentiful in Southern New York and New Jersey.

CORNUS MASCULA is a foreign species of this genus which bears edible fruit.

CRATÆGUS. (*Hawthorn.*)

There are many species in this genus, few of which attain the size of trees, as they seldom grow more than twenty feet high. The flowers are white or pale pink, resembling the apple, but smaller; fruit variable in size, sometimes not larger than a small pea, in others an inch in diameter; some are of excellent flavor, others dry and insipid; red is the most common color, but there are a number of species with yellow fruit.

All of the species produce more or less thorns, and make excellent hedges, but are exceedingly liable to be attacked by the apple-tree borer. Its seeds ripen in autumn, and should be sown at that time, for if they once get thoroughly dry they will not grow; but they will often remain in the ground two years before they germinate.

The following are probably the best for cultivation:

CRATÆGUS CORDATA (*Washington Thorn*).—Leaves broadly ovate; flowers small; fruit not larger than peas; bright red; tree fifteen to thirty feet high. Virginia and Kentucky.

CRATÆGUS TOMENTOSA (*Pear Thorn*).—Leaves large, oval, sharply toothed; flowers large; fruit crimson, sometimes an inch in diameter, sprightly flavor, edible; common in the Northern and Western States. There are several varieties of this species, some of which have yellow or yellowish-white fruit, with a very agreeable flavor.

CRATÆGUS CRUS-GALLI (*Cockspur Thorn*).—Leaves deep green, shining, very thick; fruit bright red, small; one of the handsomest native species; tree fifteen to twenty-five feet high.

The double-flowering varieties are usually budded on some one of our native kinds.

DIOSPYRUS VIRGINIANA. (*Persimmon.*)

Leaves ovate oblong, nearly or quite smooth; flowers

greenish yellow; fruit usually round, but sometimes long, slightly pointed, exceedingly astringent when green, but becomes soft and sweet when ripe, at which time it is generally deep orange yellow. In its more Northern limits it does not ripen until frost; farther South, it matures before, consequently it does not always require cold weather to make it eatable, as is sometimes asserted. The persimmon is variable, like most other fruits—some trees producing much better specimens than others. They are usually about an inch in diameter; but I have met with trees that produced fruit nearly two inches in length, and ripened nearly a month in advance of the general crop. It deserves to be more generally cultivated, and there is no reason why a really superb variety may not be produced from the native persimmon. The tree is quite ornamental, and grows twenty to thirty feet high. Native of New Jersey, and localities west and south.

There are several foreign species which are sometimes cultivated in this country. The Diospyrus kaki—Japan persimmon—and Diospyrus Lotus, a native of Italy, are both hardy in the latitude of New York city.

Euonymus atropurpureus. (*Burning Bush*, *Wahoo*, *Spindle Tree*, *Strawberry Tree.*)

Leaves deep green, oval oblong, somewhat pointed; young branches green, partially angled on thrifty young sprouts; flowers deep purple, inconspicuous; fruit usually four-sided, slightly winged, containing several bright crimson seeds; the pod, inclosing the seeds, is also crimson; very ornamental in autumn, when full of fruit; seeds will often remain in the ground two years before they germinate. Very common at the West, in low, wet soils; usually cultivated for ornament. There are also several other native species of smaller growth, also many foreign species and varieties, which can be found in any of the larger nurseries.

HALESIA TETRAPTERA. (*Silver-Bell Tree.*)

An exceedingly beautiful tree when in bloom; the flowers are of the purest white, bell-shape, with a long, slender stem; leaves oblong ovate, light green. Quite a tall, handsome shade tree can be made of it by trimming off the lower branches, but it usually forms a dense, conical shrub; wood is exceedingly hard and fine-grained; seed-pods are two to four-winged, and one to one and a half inches in length; ripe in fall, when the horn-like covering becomes very hard, requiring a long time in the ground to make them germinate. They will usually start in spring if sowed in the fall, but sometimes remain in the ground until the second season; it is a native of the South, but is hardy in most of the Northern States.

MORUS RUBRA. (*Red Mulberry.*)

Leaves usually heart-shaped on large trees, but of various shapes on young plants; fruit long, from three quarters to one and a half inches, and three eighths to half an inch in diameter, resembling a blackberry; very sweet, but sometimes brisk and vinous; usually a small tree, but sometimes nearly forty feet high and one foot in diameter.

The M. ALBA—White Mulberry of Europe—has also become naturalized, and found from New England to Illinois.

M. NIGRA—Black Mulberry, or English Mulberry—is sometimes cultivated, but is not so hardy as the native.

Mulberry seeds grow very readily if washed from fruit, sowed in fall, or put aside until spring; but they should not be covered too deep, as they are quite small. There are many varieties in cultivation: the one known as Downing's Mulberry is probably the best; it is propagated by budding or grafting it upon the Moretti Mulberry, or upon some other free-growing stock. Some kinds grow readily from cuttings of the ripe wood taken off in the fall; but others, like the Downing, are very difficult to propagate in this manner.

MACLURA AURANTIACA. (*Osage Orange.*)

This is a well-known hedge-plant, a native of Texas and other sections of the Southwest. The seeds are usually obtained from those sections, and if fresh, there is no difficulty in making them grow when planted in spring; but it is always best to mix them with moist sand and put them in a warm place until they begin to sprout before sowing. If the seeds are good, they will start in a few days; if not, they will become soft and rotten. By trying the seeds in this way, much labor will often be saved, as it is labor lost to sow unsound seeds. The Osage Orange seeds will keep sound for a year or two if placed under proper conditions; but this is often neglected, and much worthless seed is sold; and having had some experience in buying such, I give this hint to caution the readei not to sow poor seed even if he has been so unfortunate as to purchase it. The seed may also be sown in the fall, but in that case the sprouting must be dispensed with.

OLEA AMERICANA. (*Devil Wood, American Olive.*)

Leaves oblong lanceolate, four to six inches in length, smooth; branches light color, and as they become old are covered with small, round, wart-like knobs; flowers white in June or July; fruit nearly round, about three eighths of an inch in diameter. It is a native of the South, but hardy here; tree ten to thirty feet in height; propagated from seeds and cuttings.

OSTRYA VIRGINICA. (*Iron Wood, Hop Hornbeam.*)

A well-known small tree with very hard wood, much used by farmers for making beetles or mauls for splitting rails and wood; the seeds resemble hops, and the tree is called the Hop-tree in some sections. The seeds are ripe in August or first of September in the more Northern States and should be gathered so soon as ripe, as they commence falling soon after and are widely scattered by the wind. Plant immediately, or put in sand and keep in a cool place. The tree sometimes grows to forty feet high, but usually not more than twenty-five; a very slow grower.

PTELIA TRIFOLIATA. (*Hop Tree.*)

Quite a pretty small tree, which has been much extolled of late in consequence of the seeds possessing similar properties as the common Hop. The leaves are divided into three lobes, and are called tri-foliate, each division being oval, and somewhat pointed. The tree is a rapid grower when young, but does not become very large, usually not more than twenty feet high; seeds ripen in summer or early fall, and should be sown soon after; they are what is called winged seeds, and the membrane entirely surrounds them.

PYRUS CORONARIA. (*American Crab-Apple.*)

The wild Crab-Apple is seldom cultivated for ornament, still it is a very handsome tree, with large rose-colored flowers, and well worthy of cultivation; probably more plentiful in Wisconsin than elsewhere; seeds ripen in autumn, and should be taken from the apple and sown at that time. The fruit is rather harsh and bitter, and not as good as many of the cultivated Siberian Crab-Apples, which are even more ornamental, besides having the additional merit of being useful.

PYRUS AMERICANA (*American Mountain Ash*). — A well-known ornamental tree producing large clusters of scarlet fruit, which remain on the tree until quite late in the autumn. The fruit should be gathered and put in a box and kept moist until the pulp becomes soft so that it can be separated from the seeds. Wash off the pulp and sow the seeds in frames or in a half-shady situation, as the young plants are liable to be burned by the sun when they are small. It grows ten to twenty feet high; is abundant in Northern Wisconsin and Michigan; also common in cultivation.

There are also many European varieties, seeds of which

can be obtained of seedsmen. The Apple or Pear can be grafted on the Mountain Ash.

RHAMNUS CATHARTICUS. (*Buckthorn.*)

The common Buckthorn is often cultivated as a hedge-plant. It is a native of Europe, but has become naturalized in many parts of the country, especially in the Atlantic States. It makes an excellent hedge, and is not so thorny as to make it either difficult to trim or dangerous to work about, as with some other kinds of plants. If planted as single specimens, it will become quite a tree, and with its dark-green leaves and black berries in autumn it is quite an ornament. Its seeds are contained in a berry, and are quite hard; should be sown in fall, or kept in moist sand during winter, and if where frozen, all the better.

RHAMNUS LANCEOLATE.—This species of Buckthorn is found chiefly at the South; and as it has no thorns, it is not valuable for hedges.

R. ALNIFOLIUS is a Northern species; but it is only a small shrub.

SASSAFRAS OFFICINALE. (*Sassafras.*)

The Sassafras-tree is seldom planted for ornament; but there is no reason why it should not be introduced for this purpose, as it is a very handsome tree, and probably would be often planted if it were not for the uncertainty of making it live, it being one of the most difficult trees to transplant that we possess, having long, soft, naked roots which run very deep in the soil. If it is desirable to move them after they become large, say eight to ten feet high, they must be frequently transplanted in the nursery, so as to cause them to make fibrous roots and few long large roots. The leaves are of various shapes, sometimes entire; in others, one to three lobed. Young branches pale yellow or yellowish green. The bark on the roots is highly perfumed; wood light yellow, fine-grained, and hard; would be very valuable for cabinet-work if it could be had of large size. It is usually a small tree, but occasionally one will be found fifty feet high with a stem one to two feet in diameter. It thrives well on a deep sand or loam, but soon perishes on a wet soil. The flowers are small, deep yellow, in clusters; seeds are inclosed in a blue berry, ripen in autumn, and should be sown at that time; common from Florida to Lake Ontario in high, dry soils.

The Persea Carolinensis—Red Bay or Alligator Pear of the South—belongs to the same order of the Sassafras, and is a tree of similar size; also the Tetranthera geniculata or Pond Spice, which is found in the swamps of Virginia and southward.

They all belong to the Laurel family, and are classed under the generic name of Laurus in many of the works on Botany.

Shepherdia argentea. (*Buffalo Berry.*)

This is a small tree, a native of the far West, being found on the eastern slopes of the Rocky Mountains, chiefly on the upper Missouri and its tributaries. Its leaves are small and long, of a gray silvery color on both sides; the young branches are also of a grayish color. It is quite ornamental in appearance, especially in autumn, when loaded with its small, red, currant-like fruit, which is acid but quite agreeable. They are highly prized by many persons for tarts, pies, etc. The seeds grow very readily if planted in autumn. It forms a dense, large shrub; or if the lower branches are removed, it will grow from twenty to thirty feet high.

There is a small variety—S. Canadensis—which is found in some parts of the Northern States, usually along the more northern portions; but it is only a small shrub, with very insipid fruit.

The Shepherdias are what is termed by botanists diœcious plants—that is, one tree bears pistillate flowers and produces fruit; the other staminate flowers, and bears no fruit, but fertilizes the pistillate flowers; therefore to have trees produce fruit, it is necessary to have the two kinds in the same garden, and if in close proximity, all the better.

CHAPTER XII.

EVERGREEN TREES.

Our indigenous Evergreen trees do not offer so great pecuniary inducements for growing for timber as the deciduous; they grow as rapidly, and their wood is valuable, but it requires a longer time for the trees to attain an available size for the purposes for which they are chiefly used. The largest of our Evergreens, such as the Pine and Hemlock, are mainly used for boards, planks, and sawed timber, and for such purposes large trees are required, and to grow these, forty or more years are requisite. The value of our Evergreen forests is seldom or never appreciated, and we are very much inclined to attribute all the wealth, progress, and all that has contributed to place our country in its high and enviable position to its free institutions and liberal government; and while no one would wish to depreciate these, still I am equally certain that our noble forests have contributed largely toward elevating us to our present situation. The immigrant finds cheap, rich lands and a patronizing government; still, these would aid him but little toward making a home; he must have shelter for himself and his family, and our forests have supplied the materials, and so cheaply, that he can not only make one that is comfortable, but more or less elegant.

We may dig canals, build railroads, and set up the telegraph, but we must have wood to complete them; and so it is in every department which contributes to our national progress. Government may grant as many charters for public improvements as corporations may ask for—give away land to the landless; but take away our forest trees, and all these privileges would be worthless.

We have one kind of Evergreen tree which has contributed more to the wealth and prosperity of the country than all the gold and silver mines on the continent have or ever will.

The White Pine has contributed much material to build cottages and palaces, from Maine to the Mississippi; scarcely a dwelling, church, or other public or private building to which this tree has not contributed more or less. It has been so plentiful, that its real value has not been appreciated. Great forests of pine have been robbed of its best trees, and the others wantonly destroyed; but the time has now arrived when we begin to feel that there is a scarcity, for where only ten years since pine lumber brought only ten dollars per thousand feet, it now readily sells from forty to sixty, with no prospect of its being any cheaper. This great increase in price is not owing to the scarcity of labor, as some tell us, although it may be partially so at present; but it is mainly owing to the difficulty in getting the trees from which the lumber is made. If the price continues to advance—and there is no reason why it should not—it will be but a few years before lumber will be beyond the reach of the poor, or even the middle classes; and these will have to resort to the adobe and tile for their building materials.

As the few become wealthy, the more costly materials

are used, and brick and stone will form the bulk of all the better class of buildings; but if there is no cheap intermediate material between mud and stone, then the poor classes will have to take the former and the rich the latter, as is seen in most parts of Europe, where the two extremes of rich and poor stand out prominently.

The growth of most of our Western cities, especially along the great lakes and rivers, has been the wonder of the civilized world, and deservedly so, and their progress has been generally attributed to the cheap and productive soils in their immediate vicinity, and doubtless in a great measure this is true; but any one who has ever studied closely the more prominent elements that have contributed to make them great, has found that cheap lumber has been the greatest among them all.

Fifteen years ago, when Milwaukie and Chicago were making such wonderful strides toward becoming what they now are—opulent cities, pine and hemlock lumber could be had there for from five to ten dollars per thousand feet. At such cheap rates for building materials there was no reason why dwellings, stores, and warehouses should not spring up on every hand as if by magic. The same materials are now quadruple their former price, and those cities continue to grow for the reason that they have become rich and able to pay more. But they had the benefit of a cheap material at the beginning, and it is this start in the world which cities and nations, like individuals, require, and when once obtained, it only needs a steady hand and ordinary talent and judicious expenditures to reach the highest position in wealth.

It is certainly not among the impossibilities even for individuals to rear a pine forest to an available size in half a lifetime, and there are now thousands of acres of young pine forest from which the large trees have been taken that it would be a profitable investment to purchase and give a little care until the trees were grown to maturity or large enough for use. Pine lands are seldom of much value for farming purposes, consequently they are better suited for growing timber than for grain.

There are probably few sections of the country where any of the Evergreen trees could be grown as profitably as some of the most valuable deciduous trees, and my main object at this time is to call the attention of the farmer to the fact, that the Evergreens are the most valuable for shelter and ornament.

Retaining their foliage during winter, they afford protection at a time when it is most needed. A belt of these surrounding a farm, or such portions as are occupied by the buildings, gives a cheerful, comfortable appearance, and both man and beast will live longer and be more happy under such circumstances than when exposed to every gale, and for six months of the twelve with nothing lifelike to look upon. "But they shade so much ground and take so much strength from the soil," say many. This is true; and still, the benefits they confer are much in excess of all the damage they do. Those who would live the year round, and not appear to hybernate one half of it, but make summer perpetual, should plant Evergreens plentifully but judiciously about their dwellings and farms, not so abundantly that it will make the place dark and gloomy, but sufficient to make it look cheerful and pleasant The birds will remain with you later in autumn, and greet you earlier in spring, if you offer them a welcome and a few Evergreen trees for shelter. There is a great variety of form and shades of color among these trees, and they may be so intermingled that there will be no stiffness or monotony of appearance, but graceful outlines may be given to the most rugged and naturally ill-looking situation.

Trees give a solid, substantial appearance to a place, which no building, however pretentious, can or ever will produce. If a man goes into the country to buy a farm, he will seldom call where he sees beautiful trees surrounding the house and out-buildings, for he knows instinctively that such places are not for sale, for the owner generally thinks more of his home than money; but it is the bleak, uninviting farms that are usually *for sale.* There is no excuse at the present day for not having Evergreen trees and shrubs planted about every home in the country, no matter where it may be located or at what distance from Evergreen forests or from nurseries where such plants are grown for sale. Evergreen seeds can be had very cheaply, and our Government has wisely enacted postal laws that offer to every person an opportunity of transporting seeds to every part of the country for a mere nominal price. This arrangement has already been of immense value to the community, and we shall not be surprised if in its effects it proves of more real benefit to the country than the results of all the labors of the Agricultural Bureau of the Department of the Interior—unless that is conducted differently than it has been in years past

—while instead of being a tax on the Government it is a source of revenue. Sixteen cents a pound pays well, being about the same as charged for freight by express companies.

A package weighing one pound can be sent by mail from New York to Minnesota for sixteen cents, and if that pound be Norway or Hemlock Spruce, it will contain at least 20,000 seeds—enough to grow trees sufficient to surround a half dozen ordinary farms. The original cost of the seeds will probably be three dollars. Those who can not afford to purchase even this amount, could at least buy a twenty-five-cent package, which would produce with very little care more Evergreen trees than can now be found in many thickly settled towns in the Eastern as well as Western States.

All of our largest dealers in seeds keep the most common as well as many of the rare varieties of Evergreen seeds for sale, and will be happy to deliver them to you through the post-office free of expense of transportation.

The most costly varieties are not always the most useful, as it is scarcity, and not their intrinsic worth, that regulates the price of seeds, as it does that of most other commodities.

The seeds of Evergreen trees and shrubs are, as with deciduous trees, of various forms and structure. Some are very small, as in the Arborvitæ, while others are large and nut-like, as in some of the Pines. Many are light, and have thin membraneous wings; these are usually widely distributed by the winds when they fall.

Very few of the Evergreen seeds are what are usually

termed delicate seeds, for though small they retain their vitality for a comparatively long time. Most of them may be kept in any cool, dry place during winter without receiving any apparent injury. There are some kinds which will retain their vitality under proper conditions for twenty or thirty years, while others will not germinate after the first season.

The germinating power of all seeds is more or less weakened by age, consequently it is always best to procure them as fresh as possible, and not delay the planting longer than is absolutely necessary.

As many of the coniferous Evergreens shed their seeds soon after the cones are mature, it is often necessary to gather them before these open, and it is always best to be a little in advance of the time than to be too late. If the cones are not fully ripe in appearance, the seeds usually will be, or they will ripen if left in the cones after they are gathered. A few years since, when the great tree of California (Sequoia gigantea) was first discovered, a friend sent me a branch with some six cones attached for a cabinet specimen, and although it was taken from the tree before the cones were fully matured, they ripened sufficiently for growth, and I succeeded in starting two hundred of them. I mention this circumstance to show that it is not always requisite to have seeds appear to be fully ripe to insure their growth; in fact, some kinds will grow more readily if gathered before they are ready to fall than after. Some kinds may be safely sown in open seed-beds; but, as a rule, all plants are benefited by a partial shade when young, especially when we have dry, hot weather in summer. It is also necessary in the Northern States to protect them in winter for the first year or two.

TRANSPLANTING EVERGREENS.

The best time to transplant Evergreens is still, as it always has been, a debatable point, and probably will continue to be, so long as we have men in the profession who prefer to discuss a theory than to settle the question by practice. There is not a month in the year, nor a week in the month, that has not been decided to be the very best time for transplanting Evergreens, and probably there is truth in all theories, when put in practice in particular locations and countries. But specific local rules are not generally useful. Still, with all the elaborate essays and scientific acumen which have been displayed by theoretical as well as practical horticulturists upon this subject, nurserymen go on transplanting their thousands and tens of thousands every year with perfect success, regardless of that particular time which some learned essayist has pointed out.

The truth of the matter is, that it only requires a little common sense and care to perform the operation with success; and while the theoretical man is waiting for a proper time, or searching with scientific reasons for particular days, the practical man transplants his trees, *does it well*, and excels the would-be scientist in the end.

Evergreen trees have their periods of growth and rest, the same as others; and every one knows that the best time to transplant trees is when they are dormant—that is, not growing. Trees are seldom completely at rest, for they require moisture even during winter, for a partial exhalation is going on from the buds and smaller branches of trees upon which there are no leaves; and this loss of moisture must be supplied mainly through the roots, consequently it becomes necessary to keep them in a position where the required amount of moisture can be obtained; if not, the tree soon becomes dry and dead.

Evergreens probably exhale more from their leaves during winter than deciduous trees do through their buds; and this is one cause why, in very cold climates, it is injudicious to move evergreens in the fall, thereby separating the roots from the soil to which they had formed a connection by growth; not being able to form another before cold weather, they perish for the want of moisture alone. When Evergreens can be moved with a large ball of earth attached, it may be done at almost any time. In mild climates, where the soil does not freeze deeply, the fall is a safe and suitable time; but in the more Northern States this operation should be deferred until spring, unless it is done early in fall so that new roots may be emitted before cold weather.

Spring is the time chosen by our nurserymen for transplanting Evergreens, and they usually begin so soon as the ground has become sufficiently dry and settled to work easily and continue until the trees begin to make a growth. Some say the later the better; but this assertion is like many others, it being founded upon convenience; and because evergreens *can* be transplanted later than many other trees, it is usually delayed; and to give a plausible excuse for the delay, it is said to be the best time. If planted early, the ground becomes settled about their roots, and new fibers will be emitted by the time they are required to absorb plant-food to assist in the growth of the branches.

There is one thing about which it may be well to caution those who have no experience in this line, and that is, Evergreens of all kinds are very sensitive in regard to having their roots exposed to the sun and winds, much more so than deciduous trees when denuded of leaves. This is another evidence of the fact, that Evergreens do exhale moisture through their leaves when not making a growth. Never let the roots of Evergreens become dry, as it is almost sure death to them. If they are to be transported to any distance, take them from the ground and immediately cover their roots with some material that will exclude currents of air and retain moisture. Sometimes trees will live that have had their roots considerably dried, but it will take years for them to regain that vigor they formerly possessed. We see, in traveling through the country, more sickly-looking Evergreens, and hear more complaint about making such trees live, than we do in almost any branch of Horticulture; and though I would not screen those who neglect their plants or fail to see that they are properly planted, still I think that nurserymen, as a general thing, are more careless of the manner in which they take up Evergreens and pack them, than with other trees; or, in other words, they give them the same chance to live that they do their pear and apple trees, and no more, while they well know that they are more easily destroyed. I have been into large, and what are called well-conducted nurseries, and seen a score of men digging up Evergreen trees, in a dry, windy March or April day, and the earth was shaken from the roots, and then they were strewn over the ground and allowed to remain there until the packers were ready to receive them, which might be that day, and perhaps not until the next.

When Evergreens or other trees are transplanted from one's own seed-beds or nursery, a moist cloudy day can be chosen, and as much time given as required. If the soil is light, then it is best to pack it firmly around the roots so that too much air can not reach them; and if the soil is dry, and rain does not soon follow, give the soil a good soaking so that it will fill all the interstices between the roots. But watering trees, as a general thing, is useless, especially if planted in the early spring. I know it is more or less recommended in all books on gardening; but who ever saw a nurseryman watering trees? I am quite certain that I have never had occasion to water a dozen in a constant practice of nearly twenty years, and I believe that my success in making trees live is at least equal to the average.

TRIMMING EVERGREENS.

Evergreens seldom require pruning, except when some particular shape is required; but they will bear the knife as well as other trees, and it will often resuscitate a feeble specimen where good culture has failed to do it. Those varieties which can be taken up with a ball of earth, or with the roots almost entire, will need little or no pruning; but there are other kinds which will be benefited by reducing their branches. Small trees are always preferable to large ones for transplanting, and they will often outgrow them and become larger trees in five years than those that have attained a large size when transplanted.

TRANSPLANTING FROM FORESTS.

In some portions of the country very handsome Evergreens may be obtained from the forests; and when these can be carefully taken up with some soil adhering to their roots, they will often do well. But usually trees that have come up from seeds, and have not been transplanted, are difficult to make live, especially when taken from a shady situation and placed in an exposed one. Still, it is desirable to make the trees from our forests grow in our gardens, and the chances of success will warrant the labor of trial; and if small specimens are selected for the purpose, good results will often be obtained. When such trees are planted, it is best to cover the soil about them with leaves or some kind of mulch, so that it may be kept moist.

EVERGREEN TREES.

ABIES. (*Spruce, Fir.*)

This species contains several of our most beautiful as well as most valuable cone-bearing trees. They are all hardy, and found quite common in various sections of our Northern States; seeds small, with persistent wings; all ripen in fall, and must be gathered in the cones.

ABIES BALSAMEA (*Balsam Fir*).—Leaves narrow, and about an inch long; cones three to four inches long; tree tall and slender; bark with numerous blisters, from which the well-known Balsam Fir—or Canada Balsam—is taken; wood is of little value; grows naturally in a wet soil, and is of little beauty when cultivated, except when young. By the time the tree is ten years old, the lower branches die, and it becomes a tall, spindling, ill-looking tree.

ABIES FRAZERI (*Double Balsam*). — Very similar to the last, but the leaves are more numerous and the cones smaller; not worth cultivating where there are so many that are better.

ABIES CANADENSIS (*Hemlock Spruce*).—This is the most beautiful native evergreen we possess. It has a most graceful habit, with light, elegant, and delicate foliage, and branches which no one who admires an evergreen can fail to appreciate; leaves flat, dark green above and silvery underneath, little less than an inch in length; cones small, about three quarters of an inch long. The timber is coarse-grained, well known. It grows best on deep loams and stony soils; sometimes found in swamps, but seldom of large size. A light, dry soil is preferable, and a heavy clay the very last place it should be planted in, as on such it is quite tender, being often winter-killed even in this latitude, while it grows naturally hundreds of miles to the north. The tree attains a great height and size—often one hundred and twenty-five feet, and stem five to six feet in diameter.

ABIES NIGRA (*Black Spruce, Double Spruce, Red Spruce*).—Leaves three quarters of an inch long, deep green, thickly set on the branches; cones from an inch to an inch and a half long; tree an erect conical grower with stout curved branches, variable in appearance; sometimes the leaves are dark green, in others reddish or light yellow green. It is quite large, and its wood similar to hemlock, but more firm.

ABIES ALBA (*White or Single Spruce*).—Very similar to the last; but the general appearance of the tree when young is lighter colored; it loses its beauty with age; cones slightly longer than the Red Spruce, and more firm. These last two varieties should give way to that more beautiful European variety the

ABIES EXCELSA (*Norway Spruce*).—This is a magnificent tree, and succeeds in almost any good rich soil; it grows very rapidly, and retains its beautiful proportions until of great age; trees of fifty or more feet in height are quite common in the old gardens throughout the Eastern States, as well as in some of the Western. Seeds are always to be had of our seedsmen, and are easily grown in frames.

Some of the new varieties which have been lately discovered among the Rocky Mountains will no doubt be acquisitions to this class of Evergreen trees. Several of these grow to an immense height, often over two hundred feet high. Trees of most of our far Western varieties are to be had from our largest nurseries, but at very high prices. The cones of some of these trees are really wonderful in their structure, as well as beautiful.

The following give promise of being hardy, even in the Northern States:

ABIES BRACTEATA (*Leafy-coned Silver Fir*), found in Upper California and in Oregon. I have received cones of this from near the Columbia River, and without doubt it grows much farther North.

ABIES NOBILIS (*Noble Silver Fir*), also from the mountains of Upper California.

ABIES GRANDIS (*Great Silver Fir*), from Oregon, where it grows to an immense size; some specimens have been found nearly three hundred feet high.

There are also many other varieties of Evergreens belonging to this genus that are well worthy of cultivation, but none that will give more general satisfaction than the Norway Spruce and Hemlock; these are the two best of those that have been extensively tried.

Some new species from the Pacific coast promise to be acquisitions, but they are as yet scarce; whether they will be adapted to general cultivation in our Northern States remains yet to be learned.

CUPRESSUS THYOIDES. (*White Cedar.*)

Leaves very small, compressed, four rows on each side of the small branches, rather light green, becoming dull yellowish green in winter; cone very small, about a quarter of an inch in diameter; tree grows fifty to sixty feet in height; heart-wood red, fine-grained, and very durable; common in swamps in Eastern States; seeds ripen in autumn. It can also be grown from cuttings placed in frames early in autumn, same as directed for Arborvitæs.

A new species of Cypress from Northern California (Cupressus Lawsoniana) promises to be a very beautiful tree; and should it prove hardy, it will be well worthy of the attention of all lovers of beautiful trees.

JUNIPERUS. (*Juniper.*)

Well-known trees and shrubs, very common in most of the Eastern States where there are dry, sterile soils. They are all quite variable in appearance in the different sections in which they grow; the most beautiful forms are seen along the banks of the North River, where they grow among the rocks of the Palisades.

JUNIPERUS COMMUNIS (*Common Juniper*).—Leaves in threes, awl-shaped, prickly pointed, bright green, becoming dull rusty brown in winter; berries dark purple; usually low-spreading shrubs.

JUNIPERUS VIRGINIANA (*Red Cedar*).—Leaves much crowded, spreading, awl-shaped, prickly; trees of various shapes, sometimes long, pointed, conical, others low spreading; berries small, covered with a blue bloom; should be sown in autumn, or mixed with muck or leaf mold and placed in the open ground until they begin to germinate, which they will seldom do until the second spring after being gathered. The Red Cedar wood is well known as one of the most durable, as well as one of the slowest in growth. A short time since I cut a tree that was only three inches in diameter, but its annular rings showed that it was fifty-seven years old. In rich soils they will grow more rapidly.

There is a dwarf variety of Juniper (J. humilis) which is a low-spreading shrub, found along the North River and northward, and probably in many other sections of the country.

Some of the foreign species are more ornamental than our native species. The more common of these are the

J. Suecia (Swedish Juniper) and J. Hibernica (Irish Juniper). They are both very handsome, long, slender, conical-growing small trees, which give a very pleasant effect when interspersed in a group of larger-growing kinds.

The Junipers may all be grown from seeds, or from cuttings made in September or October and put in frames; but these should be covered with glass, so that the air can be kept confined and more heat retained than in the open frames. The frames should be partially shaded until the cuttings are rooted; also covered so that the ground will not be frozen in winter. Seeds are the safest method for those who have had no experience in propagating under glass. The nurserymen propagate the Junipers from green-growing wood taken off in the early part of summer; these are placed in hot-beds or in a propagating-house.

Pinus. (*Pine.*)

The Pines are among the most useful or ornamental trees that we possess, as it is from these that we derive our best lumber for building, such as siding, flooring, and general finishing of inside as well as outside work. Probably nine tenths of all the dwelling-houses in the country outside of our large cities are covered with pine shingles. Besides furnishing such vast quantities of lumber, the Pines of our Southern States furnish immense quantities of fuel, pitch, tar, resin, and turpentine; and so great is the production of these last-named articles, that we have exported in a single year more than a million dollars' worth, besides the vast quantities used at home.

The Pines are more or less difficult to transplant, as they

produce but few small fibrous roots; but this is partially obviated when they are grown in nurseries and frequently transplanted while young. The leaves are more or less long and slender, and grow in clusters of two to five, inclosed in a sheath at the base. Fig. 43 shows the leaves, natural size, of the Jersey Pine (Pinus inops). The leaves and cones are the two most prominent characteristics that

Fig. 43. Fig. 44. Fig. 45.

I shall use in describing the following species. The trees all blossom in spring; but it requires two years for the cones to mature; seeds winged.

Fig. 44 shows a seed of Pinus rigida, natural size, two of these being produced at the base of each scale of the cone. The cones should be gathered so soon as they mature, and be spread out where they will dry; this causes them to open and allow the seeds to fall out. Sow the seeds in frames or in a shady place, either in fall or spring. Fig. 45 shows a young pine as it appears when it first comes above ground; at this time they are very delicate, and require much care to prevent them from being burned by the sun or destroyed by giving too much water.

Pinus Banksiana (*Northern Scrub Pine*). — Leaves short, stout, rigid, in twos; cones one to two inches long, scales not pointed; a small tree or large shrub, of no value.

Pinus inops (*Jersey Scrub Pine*).—Leaves two to three inches long, in twos; cones obovate conical, two to three inches long, scales tipped with a sharp, stout thorn about one sixteenth of an inch in length; tree quite handsome when young, if grown in good soil, but becoming straggling when old or when grown in poor, dry, sterile hills and barrens, where it is usually most common; generally a small tree, but occasionally a group will be found that are forty to fifty feet high; New Jersey and southward.

Pinus pungens (*Table Mountain Pine*).—Leaves stout, two to three inches long, in twos; cones same form as the last, but double the size; tree of small size, seldom over fifty feet; found in Virginia and along the Blue Ridge to Alabama, also in some parts of North Carolina, as I have received cones from the latter State several years since, where it was said to be quite abundant on the high tablelands.

Pinus resinosa (*Red Pine*).—Leaves long, somewhat cylindrical, five to six inches, in twos, very dark green; cones conical, two inches long, scales not pointed; a large tree, common in the Northern States. In Northern New York, and perhaps elsewhere, it is called Norway Pine.

Pinus mitis (*Yellow Pine*).—Leaves long and slender, three to five inches, usually in twos, but sometimes threes; cones oblong conical, two inches long, scales tipped with very small prickles; New England, New Jersey, and southward; fifty to sixty feet high; wood fine-grained and valuable.

Pinus glabra (*Smooth-leaved Pine*).—There is some doubt about this being a distinct species. Chapman, in his "Botany of the Southern States," describes it as such. Leaves three to four inches long, in twos; cones two inches

Fig. 47.

Fig. 46.

long. It is called Spruce Pine at the South; and is probably only a variety of the last. I have cones of both of these species, but can see no difference between them.

PINUS RIGIDA (*Pitch Pine*).—Leaves three to six inches long, in threes, rather flat, somewhat twisted, as shown in fig. 46; cones oval, sometimes slightly conical, two to three inches long, scales tipped with a short, stout, recurved spine. Fig. 47 shows a cluster of the cones, natural size, at the end of the first summer. These were fertilized by the staminate flowers in spring, and remained almost stationary, enlarging but little during the entire season.

Fig. 48.

The next spring they enlarge very rapidly, and are of full size by the first of July. Fig. 48 shows one of the cones, natural size. These cones adhere to the tree very tenaciously, and cones ten years old can be found in abundance on the old stems and branches. The cones of this species, and probably many others, are produced on the new wood, making their appearance about the first of June. As the new growth proceeds, the cones are carried forward, as it were, so that when the shoot has finished its growth, the cones will be found about midway between the base and terminal point. Generally there will be lateral branches produced just above the cones, appearing as though produced on the terminal point of the previous year's growth. Sometimes two sets of cones will form on the same shoot, one several inches above the other. I have one before me now (June 20th, 1866); the first set on this season's growth is six inches from the base; the next eight inches above; in both cases there are no leaves on the stem for an inch or more above the cones, leaving a bare spot at the point where the cones are produced. It is a large tree, with resinous wood. New England to New Jersey and southward.

PINUS TŒDA (*Old Field Pine, Loblolly Pine*).—Leaves very long and slender, six to ten inches, in threes; cones three to five inches long, scales with short, straight spine; tree from sixty to one hundred feet high; Virginia and southward; not hardy at the North.

PINUS SEROTINA (*Pond Pine*) and P. AUSTRALIS are both Southern species that are very similar to the last; of no value for cultivation at the North.

PINUS STROBUS (*White Pine, Weymouth Pine*).—Leaves slender, dark green, three to six inches long, five in a sheath—fig. 49; cones four to six inches long, usually pendulous, scales thin, not pointed, open early in fall or winter, the seeds soon falling; tree of great size, sometimes one hundred and seventy feet high, very straight. This tree furnishes the immense quantities of white-pine lumber so well known throughout the country. It is a handsome ornamental tree of rapid growth. The young trees as they are generally found in the forests have comparatively few branches, and the tree is not dense enough to be handsome, but can be made so by severely shortening all the leading shoots.

Fig. 49.

In some sections of the country the young trees are infested with a species of bark-louse (coccus); it is covered with a white downy substance, which makes it quite conspicuous and readily detected as it fastens upon the stem and branches. A strong solution of whale-oil soap, or one pound of potash to six quarts of water, applied to the infested parts will usually destroy them. A very convenient remedy, where only the stem and larger branches are infested, is a piece of common hard soap fastened in the branches above the insects; every rain will dissolve a portion of this, which is carried down and over the insects. The young lice when first hatched are so delicate that the least particle of soap kills them, and they can neither live nor multiply on bark that is washed every rain with a solution of soap.

There are a great number of species of this genus which

are native of different parts of the Old World; many of them are perfectly hardy in our Northern States. Seeds of several of the best and most common kinds are annually imported by the seedsmen. The Pinus Cembra (Swiss Stone Pine), Pinus Corsica (Corsican Pine), Pinus Austriaca (Austrian Pine), and Pinus Sylvestris (Scotch Pine) are quite common, and to be found in all large nurseries. These and several other species are well worthy of being extensively cultivated.

There are also many species that have been discovered on the Pacific coast and among the Rocky Mountains, but as yet they are rather scarce, and their true character as to hardiness is not fully known.

SEQUOIA GIGANTEA. (*Giant Sequoia.*)

This is the largest-growing evergreen tree known on this continent, and perhaps in the world, there being specimens now growing in California which are nearly if not quite four hundred feet high, with stems twenty to thirty feet in diameter. The leaves resemble the Arborvitæs, the cones are oval and about two inches long, scales thick, pointless; seeds small, winged on all sides; wood valuable, somewhat similar to red cedar; tree of very rapid growth, but unfortunately not sufficiently hardy for general cultivation at the North, although in protected situations it grows as far north as Central New York; not fully tested.

THUJA OCCIDENTALIS. (*Arborvitæ.*)

In many portions of the country this is called Cedar;

leaves very small and compressed, resembling small scales; cones small, not more than half an inch long; scales thin, paper-like, light yellowish; seeds small, winged all round; ripe in fall, and may be kept until spring before sowing. Fig. 50 shows two cones of natural size and one of the seeds. It also grows readily from cuttings planted in frames early in autumn and protected from frost in winter. In making cuttings, it is best to take the young wood with a small portion of the old wood attached. The soil in which they are planted should be at least one half sand or sandy loam, and the remainder a good, well-decomposed leaf mold, or other old and rich soil. If planted in September or early October, and kept from freezing, they will usually be rooted by the first of May following, even when no glass is used for coverings. They should be shaded from the direct rays of the sun until winter sets in, then covered sufficiently to keep out the frost. Transplant the next spring. (See page 32.) It is a tree of small size, seldom over thirty feet.

Fig. 50.

The Arborvitæs are very numerous, and there is scarcely any country in the northern portion of our globe that does not furnish us with one or more species of this tree. Botanists have divided them into two classes—those which produce wingless seeds are called Biota, and to this class belong what is known as the Chinese Arborvitæ (Biota Chinensis), Tartarian Arborvitæ (Biota Tartarica), and many varieties which have been produced from their seeds. The Siberian Arborvitæ, which is so well known among us, has winged seeds, and properly belongs to the Thujas although generally classed among the Biotas in nurserymen's catalogues. This latter species has a very compact habit and is of slow growth, but perfectly hardy; it is a general favorite, and deservedly so. It is not improbable that this species may yet be found on our Northwest coast, as Arborvitæs are quite common there, and several new species have been sent from that locality, and are now being cultivated by our nurserymen. I have received cones and branches from the north of Oregon that are not distinguishable from the Siberian. It may be that the species known as the Siberian is nothing more than a sport from our common species. It is certainly a very near relation.

I could readily add many other species of Evergreen trees indigenous to the United States and Territories, but enough have been named to give sufficient variety for ornamenting any place, however extensive; besides, those that I have mentioned are well known, and more easily obtained than those that have been omitted.

CHAPTER XIII.

EVERGREEN SHRUBS.

To complete a structure after the more bulky portions have been put together is often more difficult and requires more taste and skill than it did to lay the foundation and rear the building; and so it is with planting a group, grove, or belt of trees, for in a few years they lift high their heads, and often leave their naked stems exposed to view, as well as allow the winds to pass where we would wish it stayed.

To avoid this, it is well to plant small shrubs which never grow to any considerable height, but keep within reach of pruning shears and knife. Some of our native evergreen shrubs are the most beautiful of any known, and all are worthy of a place in grove or garden.

By planting the smaller-growing evergreens among those of larger growth we can give a more pleasing effect to the group, as they will fill up the open spaces, tone down the tall and rugged, and give a solid and firm appearance even to the small group or narrow belt.

Many of those which I have named among the trees, such as the Arborvitæs and Junipers, may be used in place of those that are naturally small shrubs, or for planting alongside of those of tall growth, and by keeping them close-pruned they will never exceed a few feet in height; but among those we designate as shrubs there are some that produce such beautiful flowers, that to pass them by would be like passing diamonds and picking up iron when looking for ornaments.

ANDROMEDA FLORIBUNDA.—Leaves lanceolate, pointed, about two inches long; flowers in dense racemes, pure white, somewhat urn-shape, about three eighths of an inch long; a beautiful, slow-growing evergreen shrub, native of the mountains of Virginia and southward. It is quite hardy in most of the Northern States, but is not very plen tiful in cultivation, probably owing to its slow growth and the difficulty experienced by our nurserymen in propagating it. It may be grown from seed, the same as other evergreens, also from layers; but the best way is to grow it from green cuttings in a propagating-house or hot-beds. It is well worthy of more extensive cultivation.

ANDROMEDA POLIFOLIA. — Leaves lanceolate, smooth, thick, with a revolute margin, white beneath; a small shrub, seldom two feet high; grows in cold, wet soils; not so handsome as A. floribunda.

ARCTOSTAPHYLOS UVA-URSA (*Bearberry*).—A low, trailing shrub with thick evergreen leaves and red fruit, common on rocky, barren hills in New Jersey and westward; propagated from seed, layers, or from green cuttings.

BERBERIS AQUILIFOLIUM (*Mahonia. Evergreen Barberry*).—Leaves pinnate, with sharp prickles; berries blue, remaining on the bush until mid-winter; a very pretty shrub from Oregon; succeeds well in the shade; propagated by layers or cuttings of the young wood.

BUXUS (*Bo*).—Although we have no indigenous plants

of this genus, still we have cultivated some of the species for so long a time that they have become almost or quite naturalized in many of the Eastern States. All the varieties are quite hardy, especially if grown where they are partially shaded.

We often require small evergreen shrubs that will grow and thrive in the shade, and there is none more suitable for that purpose than the various kinds of Box. They can be had in great variety in almost any of the larger nurseries, and are propagated from cuttings of the ripe wood taken off in the autumn or early spring and planted in sandy soils, or from green cuttings placed under glass.

CASSANDRA CALYCULATA (*Leather Leaf*).—Leaves oblong, flat; flowers white in the axils of the upper leaves; a low, branching shrub producing an abundance of small flowers in early spring; common in bog grounds, but thrives in dry soils when cultivated; propagated from cuttings of the roots. It is also known under the name of Andromeda calyculata.

ILEX OPACA (*Holly*).—Leaves oval, flat, with uneven margins, with small spines; flowers small, yellow; berries bright red; a very handsome large shrub with beautiful glossy leaves; common in most of the Eastern States. Small plants can be usually found in the woods or in the open fields, and if carefully taken up can be made to grow very readily. A moist time in the early spring is the most suitable for transplanting. The Hollies all thrive well in the shade, and deserve more attention than they have heretofore received in this country. They may also be grown from seed and from green cuttings.

ILEX CASSINE (*Cassena. Yaupon*).—Leaves lanceolate, oval, one to two inches long, not spiny, but simply serrate; native of Virginia and southward. The celebrated Yaupon tea of the Carolinas is made of the leaves of this plant; hardy in protected situations at the North.

ILEX MYRTIFOLIA (*Small-leaved Holly*).—Leaves very narrow, and only an inch long, sharply serrate; flowers singly or in small clusters; Virginia and southward along the coast.

ILEX DAHOON (*Dahoon Holly*).—Leaves oblong lanceolate, serrate, two to three inches long, margins mostly revolute; swamps of the Carolinas and southward.

ILEX GLABRA (*Inkberry*).—Leaves oblong, slightly wedge-shaped, smooth, dark green; flowers small, white; a low, slender shrub of no great beauty; common from Massachusetts to Florida along the coast; Prinos glabra of the old botanists.

KALMIA. (*American Laurel.*)

The Kalmias are greatly admired in Europe, and no gentleman's garden would be thought to be complete without its group of American Laurels. But here, in its native country, it is neglected and passed by as a thing to be almost despised, simply because it is *common* in some localities. Occasionally we see a group in some gentleman's ground, but in most cases I fear that it is only found there because the owner imported it, supposing he was getting some foreign plant. This false taste, which admires a plant that comes from abroad more than one that is native, is, I fear, too prevalent among us.

There is certainly no evergreen shrub more beautiful, nor one that deserves more attention, than our native broad-leaved Kalmia. It is said to be difficult to transplant, but I have not found it so even with plants twenty to thirty years old. To select plants from a thick wood for planting in an open garden is certainly not judicious, but the plants should be placed in a similar soil and situation as the one from which they were taken. It is also best to transplant just after a rain, and take them up with as much soil adhering to their roots as possible. If but few roots are saved, then it is best to cut them back severely when planted, as there is no evergreen shrub which produces new shoots more freely when cut back than the Laurel. The Laurels may be grown from seed, but they grow very slowly, and it will require several years for the seedlings to become plants of any great size. Layers made of the young wood emit roots quite freely.

Kalmia latifolia (*Mountain Laurel*).—Leaves oval-lanceolate, tapering to both ends, bright green; flowers pink or white, bell-shaped in large terminal clusters, produced in May and June; shrubs six to fifteen feet high; Maine to Georgia; grows in dry, rocky soils, also in poor sandy soils, although it grows more rapidly in that which is moist and deep; suitable for shady situations. It is very common in the States of Pennsylvania and New Jersey.

Kalmia angustifolia (*Sheep Laurel*).—Leaves oblong, small, light green above, pale green or whitish underneath; flowers deep rose, in small lateral clusters almost surrounding the last season's growth; plant one to three feet high;

branches slender; common on dry sandy soils in most of the Eastern States.

The Laurels are supposed in many sections to be very poisonous to sheep, and wonderful stories are in circulation as to its deleterious effects on various kinds of animals. Probably the only truth there is in these tales is the fact, that sheep when not supplied with sufficient food will eat more of the laurel leaves than their stomachs will digest, and they become rolled up in a hard ball, and by remaining in the stomach cause irritation, and then inflammation, which produces death. In such instances the Laurels, as well as other thick-leaved evergreens, become dangerous, just the same as an old boot or a lump of hair or other similar substances which sheep and cattle will occasionally eat.

KALMIA GLAUCA (*Pale Laurel*).—Leaves oblong, white, glaucous beneath, with somewhat revolute margins; flowers lilac purple, terminal, few; a small shrub, seldom more than one foot high; grows in cold peat soils in Pennsylvania and New York.

KALMIA HIRSUTA (*Rough Laurel*). — Leaves oblong, three to four inches long, smooth; flowers rose color, produced singly in the axils of the leaves on the new growth of the season; native of the swamps of the South.

LEDUM LATIFOLIUM (*Labrador Tea*).—Leaves elliptical, oblong, entire, alternate, rusty woolly underneath, with revolute margins; flowers white, quite handsome, in terminal clusters; small shrubs in cold peat bogs; blooms in June; New England and most of the Northern States, also in Canada. Another species, L. palustre, has long, narrow leaves, and is found chiefly in the more northern portion of the Canadas.

LOISELEURIA PROCUMBENS (*Alpine Azalea*).—A small, trailing evergreen shrub with small white or rose-colored flowers and small opposite elliptical leaves; propagated from layers; found in the mountains of New Hampshire.

LEIOPHYLLUM BUXIFOLIUM (*Sand Myrtle*). — Leaves about one half inch long, oval, smooth, glossy, very thick, mostly opposite; flowers terminal, in clusters, small, white, not showy; a spreading shrub, five to ten feet high.

RHODODENDRON.

The Rhododendron has been and is still admired by all civilized nations. Its flowers, foliage, and general habit command the attention of every beholder. Its name is derived from a Greek word signifying rose-tree, and there is none of the species to which the name is more applicable than to one of our native species—R. Catawbiense.

Rhododendrons are found in many portions of the globe. Tartary, China, Siberia, Japan, Italy, Caucasus, and many other portions of the Eastern world, contribute different species to ornament the groves and gardens of civilized man, whether he dwells in city or country.

Although the Rhododendron is so much admired at the present time, still there was a day when it was condemned in no measured terms. In the time of the ancient Romans it was supposed to be a very poisonous plant, and deadly to all kinds of animals, but a counter-poison to man, especially against the bite of serpents. Even the honey which the bees gathered from the flowers was said to be poisonous; and the poor people of the regions where the Pontic Rhododendron was plentiful were much perplexed on the account of their tribute of honey being refused by the Roman government. The prejudice against this plant was prevalent as late as 1568, for Dr. Turner says that he did not wish it introduced into England, for although beautiful without, that within it was a ravenous wolf and a murderer. But the dreadful character given it did not prevent its introduction, and at the present time English gardens derive their greatest beauty from their groups of Rhododendrons. No garden is complete, nay, scarcely beautiful, without a few plants at least of this splendid evergreen shrub.

Our indigenous species are equally as beautiful as those from foreign countries, and they can be had from the woods and fields of many portions of the Northern and Southern States. The same care is requisite in transplanting them as with the Kalmia, and no more. They are also easily grown from the seed, which ripens in autumn. Sow in frames the same as with other evergreens. Nurserymen propagate them in various ways, such as cuttings, layers, grafting the scarce varieties on the more common, etc.

Rhododendron maximum (*Great Laurel*).—Leaves obovate oblong, acute, smooth on both sides, deep green, six to ten inches long; flowers in terminal clusters, white or pale rose color, marked with greenish yellow, slightly spotted with red; shrubs six to twenty feet high; New England to Georgia, but more common along the banks of streams in Western New Jersey and Pennsylvania.

RHODODENDRON CATAWBIENSE (*Rose Bay*). — Leaves oval or oblong, rounded at both ends, smooth, dark green above, and pale green beneath, three to five inches long; flowers lilac purple, in large, round terminal clusters; very showy, and the most beautiful native species. Grows from three to six feet high, and native of the Alleghanies and to the southward along the mountains.

RHODODENDRON LAPPONICUM (*Lapland Rose*).—Leaves very small, elliptical, obtuse, dotted on both sides; branches with rusty scales; flowers violet purple, bell-shaped, in small clusters; a low-spreading shrub, three to six feet high; in Northern New York and eastward to Maine.

RHODODENDRON PUNCTATUM (*Spotted Laurel*).—Leaves elliptical, acute at both ends, two to five inches long, smooth, with small resinous globules on the under side; flowers rose color, spotted within, in large clusters; shrub four to six feet high; North Carolina and southward.

TAXUS CANADENSIS (*American Yew*, *Ground Hemlock*). —Leaves linear, green on both sides; seed a round, bright red berry very ornamental. A low, wide-spreading shrub, usually found in rocky situations in the shade; propagated from layers or cuttings; seeds seldom grow until they have been in the ground two years; a handsome evergreen shrub found on the Alleghanies and to the northward along the banks of streams. Common on the highlands of the Hudson River.

There are many more evergreen shrubs and plants that might be added, but the foregoing will be found to contain the most beautiful of our native species, and a sufficient number to make every farmer's home in the country as cheerful and beautiful as the most refined taste could desire.

It is certainly not because there is any scarcity of material that makes many of our farmers' homes look so desolate and uninviting; but it is because there is a want of energy and a proper cultivated taste.

The farmer above all others should plant trees, shrubs, and flowers about his home, for he can obtain them from the woods and fields without money or price. Let him once begin with a proper spirit, and the labor of arranging, planting, etc., will become a pleasant recreation instead of an irksome toil. I do not believe that American farmers, as a class, possess less taste for the beautiful than those of some other countries, for I know many, very many, most beautiful homes among the poorer class of farmers, as well as the rich. But there are too many who never plant a tree or shrub for ornament, and the taste for the beautiful in nature is not so general as it should be, to make our country foremost in all that will elevate and bless mankind.

RECAPITULATION.

In the following list I have endeavored to select only the most valuable of those trees mentioned in the preceding pages, noting their particular points of excellence.

Acer saccharinum (*Hard Maple*).—Tree of rather slow growth, but the wood very valuable for fuel.

Acer dasycarpum (*Silver Maple*).—Not equal in quality to the last, but much more rapid in growth.

Castanea vesca (*Chestnut*).—A rapid grower, and very valuable for posts, stakes, and other similar purposes; very durable.

Carya (*Hickory*).—The Hickories are all of rather slow growth, but valuable, while young, for hoop-poles. They also make the very best fuel when old. The Carya tomentosa is probably the most profitable to grow for its timber, but is not always the toughest.

The Carya alba (*Shell-Bark*) and Carya olivæformis (*Pecan-nut*) produce the most valuable nuts.

Fagus feruginea (*Red Beech*).—Tree of slow growth, but will thrive on shallow, stony soils; valuable, while young, for hoop poles, and excellent for fuel and many other purposes when mature.

Fraxinus Americana (*White Ash*).—A moderately rapid grower, producing a tough and most valuable timber. This is one of the most profitable trees to grow, requiring a deep, rich soil.

FRAXINUS SAMBUCIFOLIA (*Water Ash*).—Of rapid growth, valuable for growing in low, wet soils.

LARIX COMMUNIS (*European White Larch*).—Succeeds well on dry, sandy soils, also on those that are moist and rich; of rapid growth; timber very valuable. Should be extensively cultivated near all of our large seaports.

POPULUS (*Poplar*).—There are two or three species of Poplar which might be profitably grown on the prairies for fuel, although it would not be of the best quality. The growth of all the Poplars is very rapid, and they are very readily propagated from cuttings.

QUERCUS ALBA (*White Oak*).—A slow grower, but the timber is exceedingly valuable at all ages.

QUERCUS OBTUSILOBA (*Post Oak*).—Similar to the last, but will thrive in poorer soils.

SALIX ALBA (*White Willow*).—Particularly valuable for growing on the prairies. Growth very rapid; timber of fair quality for fuel.

TAXODIUM DISTICHUM (*Cypress*).—Grows rapidly; very durable timber, excellent for posts, stakes, or for fuel.

ULMUS AMERICANA (*White Elm*). —Valuable where very tough timber is required; tree of very rapid growth; succeeds best on deep, rich, alluvial soils.

INDEX.

www.ingramcontent.com/pod-product-compliance
Lightning Source LLC
LaVergne TN
LVHW011226110826
845150LV00006B/1561

* 9 7 8 1 4 2 5 5 1 5 5 8 4 *